‹ HYMAN'S ›

The World's Most Accurate

ANTIQUES & COLLECTIBLES PRICE GUIDE

Companion Publication for

compiled by
Dr. Tony Hyman

written by
Trash or Treasure Listees

Treasure Hunt Publications
Shell Beach, California

© H.A. Tony Hyman
Fall, 1994

Where to Sell Series of books by Tony Hyman
The Where To Sell Anything and Everything Book
Where To Sell Anything and Everything by Mail
Cash For Your Undiscovered Treasures
I'll Buy That!
I'll Buy That Too!
Where to Sell It
Trash or Treasure

Books on tobacco collectibles by Tony Hyman
The World of Smoking and Tobacco at Auction
Handbook of American Cigar Boxes

Treasure Hunt Publications
PO Box 3028
Shell Beach, CA 93448

Trash or Treasure is available at discount in case lots. Custom editions can be created. Call (805) 773-6777.

Editor: Marilee Hyman, Shell Beach
Design: Steve Gussman, North Hollywood

PRINTING: 0 9 8 7 6 5 4 3 2 1   ISBN: 0-937111-04-X

Dear Reader:

Welcome to *The World's Most Accurate Price Guide*. That's quite a claim! Can we prove it? We sure can!

To find out why this price guide is different and more accurate let's start by taking a look at other general price guides on the market and how they are put together. Most price guide "values" are derived as a composite of auction results, prices being asked in shops, prices being asked in ads appearing in antiques publications, what antique dealers claim they got for an item and what collectors claim they paid for an item. Clerks type these figures into a computer which averages them. These averages are published as the "value." That's why you frequently see unrealistic values like $1,025. You know and I know that nothing actually sold at that price, so where does a price like that come from? Perhaps something like this:

New York City Madison Avenue shop $1,700
Palm Springs, CA, shop   900
Ad in *The Antique Trader Weekly*   800
Downstate Illinois auction house   700

The average of these prices is $1,025, so that amount gets printed in a price guide. When you carry your item to a local dealer and ask $1,000 for it "because that's what the book says," you will be sadly disappointed when the highest offer you receive is $300 to $500.

There is another danger in taking price guide prices as an indicator of value. Sometimes they are too low. I've talked with experts who read price guides and say, "I'll take every one I can get at that price. It's worth five times that!" Wouldn't you hate to discover your $1,025 item could have been sold for $5,000?

General price guides list artificial numbers, *not prices you will get when you sell your things.* Like the porridge in another piece of fiction, some prices are too high, some too low, and some just right. In some cases they are deliberately skewed by an author attempting to raise or lower values within a hobby. Whether or not these prices are accurate doesn't matter if all you want is a rough idea of what something you own is worth.

Unfortunately that's not good enough for most readers. People obtain copies of my buyer directories because they want to *sell* things. Value becomes important when you go to sell something. Then, the difference between $40 and $400 becomes great. That's what makes *The World's Most Accurate Price Guide* so unusual.

This is the only general price guide which tells you *how much cash someone is going to take out of their pocket and put in yours.* Not only that, **The World's Most Accurate Price Guide tells you** *who* **exactly will put that money in your pocket.**

Best of all, if your item is not in this book and you identify yourself as a reader of *Hyman's Price Guide,* **you may contact the buyer of those items and ask.** No other price guide gives you this invitation.

Finally, a useful accurate price guide!

Table of Contents

Dear Reader 3

Using price guides 6

"What's my item worth?" 10

"How much will I be paid?" 11

Contacting Buyers 13

Form letter help: Sell-A-Gram 14-15

PRICES AND BUYERS

Music Boxes, *Martin Roenigk* 16

Cookie Jars, *Kier Linn* 17

.Stoneware & Crocks, *Richard Hume* 18-19

Paperweights, *Paul Dunlop* 20-21

Cast Iron Pans, *David Smith* 22

Silverware, *MidweSterling* 23

Banks, Toys, & Clocks, *Gregory Zemenick* 24-26

Model Kits & Toys, *David Welch* 27

Toy Guns, *Jim Buskirk* 28

Robots & Motorcycles, *Chris Savino* 29

Toy Trains, *Dr. Hilly Lazarus* 30-31

Barbie Dolls, *Marl Davidson* 32

Beatles, *Jeff Augsburger* 33

Pop Culture, *Ted Hake* 34-35

Lunch Boxes, *Mark Blondy* 36

Pez & Premiums, *David Welch* 37

Comic Book/Strip Art, *Tom Horvitz* 38-39

Radios, *Gary Schneider* 40

Movie Posters, *Dwight Cleveland* 41

Magic, *Ken Trombly* 42-43

78 rpm Records, *Kurt Nauck* 44-45

Phonograph Records, *Les Docks* 46-47

Musical Instruments, *Steve Senerchia* 48

Golf, *Richard Regan* 49

Sports, *Richard Simon* 50-51

Sports, *John Buonaguidi* 52-53

Fishing Tackle, *Rick Edmisten* 54-55

Beer, *Lynn Geyer* 56-57

Cigar Boxes & Labels, *Tony Hyman* 58-59

Cigarette Lighters, *Tom O'Key* 60-61

Cowboy Items, *Lee Jacobs* 62-63

Indian Artifacts, *Jan Sorgenfrei* 64

Bottles, *Steve Ketcham* 65

Boy Scouts, *Ron Aldridge* 66-67

Marine Artifacts, *Andrew Jacobson* 68-69

Typewriters, *Darryl Rehr* 70-71

Guns & Trapping, *Ron Willoughby* 72

Ammunitions & Bombs, *Dr. Crittenden Schmitt* 73

Bossons Figures, *Don & Barbara Hardisty* 74-75

Tokens & Medals, *Rich Hartzog* 76-78

Stocks & Bonds, *Warren Anderson* 79

Books & Catalogs, *Jim Presgraves* 80

Books, *Lee & Mike Temares* 81

Other Price Guides 82-91

Special Offer to Readers 92

Ordering Blanks 93

Other Books by Tony Hyman 94-96

USING THIS PRICE GUIDE

I don't particularly like price guides. I don't believe they are needed. What an item is worth is irrelevant until I'm going to sell it, and when I'm ready to sell it, I simply call an expert, tell him or her what I have and tell them to send me a check for a fair price. Then I send the item to them. It's that easy. I find out what it's "worth" when I get my check. If you don't want to sell it, then what difference does it make what some book says it's "worth"?

But forty years buying and selling antiques and collectibles has taught me that some folks feel secure when they have a book in front of them that puts a dollar value on things. Since most price guides are so inaccurate, we put this guide together so you will know what some items are *really* worth. These prices tell you how much cash you will actually put in your pocket. No other price guide does that.

You probably won't find your item in here. You probably won't find your item in *any* guide. There are billions of items, and only a small handful are listed in guides. The advantage of using *this* guide over all others is that we provide you a name and address of someone you can actually get money from...or call or write to find out more information about similar things that aren't listed.

Each page in this guide is written by one of the expert buyers you can find in *Trash or Treasure*. Each one of these people approached writing a price guide slightly differently. Some of these folks have given you long lists with prices indicated, like most price guides. The difference is, these are *real* prices because they tell you how much money they will pay..how much you will get. In some cases, buyers have given you a range of prices. The range reflects acceptable levels of condition or minor variations in the item being priced.

Since only 100 or so items can be listed on a page, a few buyers have used the opportunity to teach you about their specialty to help you determine what you have and how much it might sell for.

SUMMARY:

Here's how we recommend you sell your collectibles:
1. **Find something you want to sell**
2. **Ask one of Hyman's guides to see who wants it**
   (see this price guide or look in Trash or Treasure)
3. **Send a letter or Sell-A-Gram** *(see pages 14-15)*
4. **Take their offer, as it will probably be accurate and fair**

USING OTHER PRICE GUIDES

Price guides have a place.

If I didn't think so, I wouldn't have gone to such great trouble to assemble this very special price guide for you.

Three different kinds of guides are available:
- (1) general,
- (2) specialty,
- (3) comprehensive specialty.

To use them, you need to understand what they are, how they are different, and what they can and can't do for you.

GENERAL GUIDES

The book you are reading right now is a "general price guide." Bigger and better known general guides include those produced each year by the Kovels and *The Antique Trader*. General guides cover a variety of topics, but no one guide can cover everything. Our guide (in its first edition) covers only a few topics. Even the giant guides with their claims of 50,000+ prices cover only a tiny handful of possible items. When you consider there have been literally billions of items manufactured that are collectible to someone, you can understand why all general guides are of limited use, particularly to amateur sellers. The truth is, most of the items you want to look up, you won't find in this book or in any general guide. After 3 to 4 years, a general guide is obsolete.

General guides are created for entry level and beginning antique and flea market dealers. They buy households and large quantities of "stuff" and use these guides to get an idea of how to price. Since they handle many thousands of items, a mistake or two (or ten or one hundred) doesn't matter much in the long haul People who buy entire estates pay so little they can afford to sell items at only a rough approximation of value. You can't afford to do that...unless of course you're terribly rich and can afford to throw away $100 bills.

After 40 years experience coast to coast, I know that many antique dealers are weekenders and amateurs...sellers of second hand goods. General price guides give them a small amount of guidance but they still make plenty mistakes. You can walk into almost any antique shop in America and find items priced for 10% to 30% of what expert buyers would be willing to pay. I've never known an expert experienced dealer who uses general price guides.

You might well ask, "Why, if experts pay so much more, don't more antique dealers sell to them?" The best dealers do. Over the years, they have cultivated a following of expert buyers to whom they sell quickly and at high prices. Dealers who use my *Where To Sell Series* say they double and triple their overall income as a result.

SPECIALTY GUIDES

Specialty guides are price guides on a single topic, like lighters, blue willow china, *Colt* pistols, matchcovers, etc. As with everything else in life, quality varies widely. Some outstanding specialty guides exist, while others can actually cause you to lose money.

To evaluate a specialty price guide look for:

(1) **Pictures**: you want pictures of all major variations of pattern and shape, as well as pictures which can help you locate and identify key elements of a particular type of item.

(2) **Lots of explanatory text:** you want examples of marks, definitions of parts of an item, history of the makers and processes involved, etc. If every collectible item in a hobby can't be priced and pictured, this text can be very useful to determine rarity, estimate value, and learn how to describe your item.

(3) **Dating information:** almost all collectibles have key identifying elements which make it possible for you to date them. Information about marks, color, form and other elements all help and should be provided.

(4) **Information about grading and condition:** condition is an integral part of valuing any collectible. The standards applied by collectors and dealers within the hobby should be explained.

(5) **Authors with solid backgrounds:** look for books by folks with no less than ten years experience. I prefer those by club officers, newsletter editors, and other people in touch with many other people in their hobby. Antiques book publishers, including some of the well-known ones, have staff "writers" whose job it is to crank out books because an item is "hot" with little regard for information. If a book doesn't contain a biography of the author, beware.

(6) **An index:** books without indexes are always of less use; when a book is small, like this guide, a table of contents may suffice.

(7) **Information on how prices are determined:** you want to know the reasons an author says, "it is worth $xxx."

If the price guide you are considering has all or most of those characteristics, it is a good investment if you want to be a collector, dealer, or picker of those items. There is no substitute for information. If you'd like to see a really bad book along side a really good one, compare *Collecting Cigarette Lighters* by Wood with the very useful *Ronson: The World's Greatest Lighter* by Cummings.

Many hundreds of specialty guides are available if you live near a large bookstore willing to stock them, or if you have access to one of the three or four mail order antique book companies. Since it is very difficult to obtain some guides, we are offering to find them for you. See pages 82-90 in this book. I regret that I have not personally read all these guides and am relying on recommendations.

COMPREHENSIVE SPECIALTY GUIDES

Comprehensive specialty guides are price guides on a single topic. In addition to all the characteristics described above, comprehensive guides make a serious effort to picture, describe, and/or price all or nearly all known items in a give collectible field.

Stamps and coins are two fields with well-known comprehensive specialty guides available. Comic books, Beatles memorabilia, *Avon, PEZ* dispensers, *Hot Wheels, Hummel, Gillette, Fostoria,* baseball cards, cigarette cards, presidential pin-back buttons, *Little Golden Books,* and Disneyana are among lesser known fields with outstanding comprehensive specialty guides.

People who are not expert do not tackle the enormous chore of compiling comprehensive specialty guides. Once completed, they typically become the "bibles" of their hobby. If you are planning to become a dealer, picker, or collector in any field, buy a comprehensive guide if one exists. These are indispensible works for anyone who plans to take a given topic seriously.

Specialty guides are the best to use, but they aren't possible for all topics. There can be no comprehensive guide to books because there have been millions upon millions of books, many of which don't even have established collector values. Cigar boxes (one and a half million different), folk art (where every piece is different), matchcovers (countless unrecorded numbers), and trade (advertising) cards are other examples of topics which can never have *comprehensive* guides, but which do have excellent specialty guides available now.

Some minor problems exist for users of specialty guides. They are aimed at a select audience of people seriously interested in a topic. As a result, they sometimes use a specialized vocabulary and assume certain knowledge on the part of their readers. Availability can be a problem. Many guides sell less than 3,000 copies nationwide, and some excellent books have total printings less than 1,000. Specialty guides can be difficult to find in public libraries. Libraries are short of funds and don't buy them because of their limited appeal.

CAUTIONS ABOUT ALL GUIDES

Price guides have limitations, the greatest one being the reader. Readers have a tendency to glance at the "price" given, close the book and think they have learned something. Even worse, they will sometimes try to act on that "knowledge." If you buy a guide, any guide, **read the introductory material.**

Keep in mind that the more rare an item, the less likely it is to be listed in a price guide. If a rare item *is* listed, it is more likely to be priced inaccurately because there are fewer examples for comparison.

A sure way to lose money is to assume the price of an item similar to yours is the price of yours. Tiny variations can be big fortunes. A single letter on a coin can mean a difference of $50,000 in your pocket. Be very careful if what you have doesn't match exactly!

"WHAT'S MY ITEM WORTH?"

No book can tell you what your item is worth, although the one you're reading right now comes as close as practical. No book can tell you because, even though collectible...even antique...you are still trying to sell second hand goods. No two second hand items are identical. The amount of money realized when something is sold depends on how, where, why, by whom and to whom it is sold.

I'd like you to get as much money as possible with a minimum of time and effort. That's what *Trash or Treasure* and this price guide are about.

The world is full of books and people who say, "Your [whatever] is worth [whatever]." But in the world of antiques and collectibles nothing has dollar value until you sell it. Only when a buyer and seller agree to a price and money changes hands is value determined. Each time something sells, its value could be more, less, or the same as the day before. In the world of second hand goods, selling is always a bit of an adventure.

For most people, setting the price is the most difficult part of selling. Selling the way I do, offers you an alternative to the hassle and guesswork of pricing.

I know very little about electric trains. If I have an electric train to sell, how can I put a price on it? I can't. Not with any accuracy. I'd be as likely to underprice it as overprice it...either give it away or not be able to sell it at all.

If I don't know enough to set a selling price, who does? An expert in electric trains, that's who. For forty years I've been dealing with experts and letting them tell me what prices they will pay me. I usually accept what they offer, but sometimes don't. I usually find I make the most money by trusting an expert to make me a fair offer. The process is usually simple, quick, and profitable.

When dealing with experts I don't even need to know exactly what I have. Their years of experience enables them to tell me in seconds what could take me weeks or months of research to learn.

It is popular these days to be cynical about honesty and to assume everyone is crooked. Fortunately, that's simply not the case. The world is full of honest, knowledgeable, helpful people, a few of whom you will meet in the pages of this book. If you deal with good people, you don't need to know an item's value to get a fair price. You don't even need to know what your item is. The Midwestern lady who got $4,800 for a crock didn't have the foggiest notion of what her item was worth, except that a local antique dealer offered "$50 or $60" for it. The honest expert she dealt with (Dick Hume, page 18) evaluated her crock with an expert's eye and paid her $4,800.

Whenever you offer something for sale, a buyer will evaluate your item in terms of scarcity, desirability and condition. Dealing with an expert buyer makes it more likely you will get an accurate assessment of what you have and a reasonable estimate of fair market value.

When a buyer makes you an offer, weigh the amount of money you will get against how much you enjoy owning the object. Also consider the satisfaction of helping a collector or researcher and the comfort of knowing your cherished item will have a caring new home. More often than not, **I accept the offer, sell and move on with my life.**

What's to keep a buyer from ripping you off? That depends on the buyer. If you are careless about who you pick, you might be cheated. You must pick carefully.

My *Where To Sell Series* and companion price guides introduce you to the people I personally sell to. In the next few pages you'll meet some of the country's top experts in their fields: men and women who write price guides, edit newsletters and are officers in collectors' clubs. Many of these people have been at their hobbies for 20 years or more. These folks have careers and reputations at stake when they do business. If they cheat you, word will get around fast. Dishonest people do not stay in business long in the world of collectibles.

Some folks claim there is a conflict of interest in having the same person evaluate and set the price. That situation can occur, but my experience is that **I get fair prices when dealing with honest people.** And I'm confident that I'm a great many dollars ahead of selling at a yard sale, flea market, or local auction.

Fast, easy, and fair. Works for me...and tens of thousands of other people. It will work for you.

HOW MUCH WILL A COLLECTOR OR DEALER PAY?

The following are generalizations. They are not meant to portray any particular dealer or group of dealers. They are based on years of experience, observation, reading, and reports from dealers themselves.

A flea market dealer usually sells lower priced goods (under $40) or sells medium priced goods (under $500) at low prices. They are seldom in a position to pay more than a few cents on a dollar. Many mall dealers (where dozens of people share stalls in warehouse-like shops) pay only slightly more.

Shop dealers come in all sizes, shapes specialties and skill levels, so generalizations are difficult. From a business standpoint, the general or semi-specialist shop must try to pay from 5% to 30% to survive in the face of high expenses. Shop owners make frequent mistakes because their experience is usually limited to a few fields. When they buy outside their specialty, they must pay low.

Auction houses exist at all levels of skill and clientele. The price you get will depend upon the quality of your item, its history, what is being auctioned the same day, when and where the auction is held, and, most important of all, who will be attracted to bid in the auction. Most sales at auctions are to dealers who will double or triple the auction price (except on very expensive items) when they sell to their customers. Prices realized at auction range from 1% to a typical 15% to 60% of what items will bring in private sale to specialists. Top flight goods will sometimes sell for 50% to 100% of value, or more.

Record prices are set at auction. Record prices are also set in private sale; those prices are not reported publically but they happen as often. Don't forget you will pay a commission to an auction house of 15% to 25% of the bid. Selling goods through an auction house does not guarantee your item will be properly identified or evaluated. Errors in evaluation and identification are a lot more frequent than the big auction houses would like you to believe. At least two good size auction houses have recently succumbed to criminal charges, legal troubles, or financial woes, so investigate any auctioneer thoroughly before turning over your goods.

A specialty dealer usually pays from 20% to 75% of an item's full retail value. It depends on how much money he has, how anxious he is to add your item to his inventory and how quickly he thinks your item will resell. The more expensive the item, the higher percentage of retail value you should expect. Specialty dealers will buy a wider range of items than will collectors. Too, it is very difficult to find specialty collectors, many of whom prefer to remain anonymous, buying their goods through specialty dealers.

Collectors tend to pay the most, between 60% and 100% (or more) of what anyone else will pay. One collector explained:

> "If I'm offered a common item, worth only $5 or $6, I'm rarely interested in paying more than a dollar or two for it, if I buy it at all. I don't want to tie up money or space with minor items. When someone offers me a $100 item, I'm willing to pay full value or even more. If it's a *very* rare item, I'm willing to set record prices to make certain I get it."

AS STRANGE AS IT MIGHT SEEM...

When dealing with specialty dealers and collectors, **high value items are much easier for you to sell than low value items.** Items have low value because everyone who wants them has them, so demand is low. It is almost impossible, for example, to sell a $20 tin can today, but you can sell a $1,000 tin can is less than five minutes. A $2 cigar box will find no takers, whereas a $200 box will sell quickly if you know the right buyer.

SUMMARY REPEATED:

Here's what you do to sell your collectibles:
1. **Find something you want to sell**
2. **Ask one of Hyman's guides to see who wants it**
   (see this price guide or look in Trash or Treasure)
3. **Send a letter or Sell-A-Gram** *(see pages 14-15)*
4. **Take their offer, as it will probably be accurate and fair**

CONTACTING BUYERS

WHO ARE THE PEOPLE WHO WROTE THIS GUIDE?

The people who wrote the prices in this book average more than 15 years experience and are well known in their fields. Many of them are full time antique dealers and auctioneers. Six are doctors, dentists or psychiatrists who have made a lifetime study of their hobby. Because they are experienced they can tell you in seconds what you have and how much cash it is likely to raise for you. The most important characteristic of the people you'll meet in this guide is that **they all have made the commitment to treat you fairly.** That's why these are the people I personally do business with.

PHONES AND FAXES

Phones are a great convenience when you want to sell in a hurry, have large quantities or have complicated things to describe.

> Always have the item in front of you when you call.
> Be conscious of time differences. If you live on the East coast, don't call California before noon.
> Don't call collect.
> If you leave a message on an answering machine, speak slowly and clearly. Include your name, phone number, best time to call, and information about why you are calling.

One of the many advantages of fax is that you can do it any time of the day or night. Since a fax is a printed piece of paper, the person on the other end can deal with it at his or her convenience, perhaps after looking up information for you etc. Fax also gives you a printed record of correspondence and agreements.

PHOTOCOPIES AND PHOTOGRAPHS

Photocopies are made with a Xerox© type machine. I suggest you make a photocopy of what you have to sell because it is the cheapest and easiest way to describe most items. Objects such as knives, small dolls, badges, medals, pipes, even pistols, will usually photocopy well enough for a buyer to know what you have. Copies are especially useful for describing china patterns and paper goods. Color copies are an unnecessary expense in most cases.

Photographs are taken with a camera. The best photos are close-ups taken with a 35mm camera. If you do not have a camera, perhaps a friend who does can take pictures for you. Polaroid and snapshot cameras frequently do not provide enough detail to be useful to a potential buyer.

SELL-A-GRAMS

Use the form found on the next two pages. You may either make Xerox© copies of it (preferably on yellow paper) or use it as a guide for providing information in a letter. Let people know you found them in this guidebook. Always include a Stamped Self-Addressed Envelope if you want a reply.

ORDER FORM

☐ The item is for sale for $ _____ plus shipping.

☐ The item is for sale. I am an amateur seller and would like you to make an offer.

☐ The item may be for sale if the price is sufficient. Would you like to make an offer?

☐ The item is not for sale, but I am willing to pay a fee to learn its value.

To assist you to evaluate the item, I am enclosing a:

☐ Sample ☐ Photocopy ☐ Photo ☐ Tracing ☐ Sketch ☐ Rubbing ☐ Nothing

This is to certify that, to the best of my knowledge, the item is genuine and as described.
Buyer has a 5 day examination period during which the item may be returned for any reason.

Signature: _____ **Date:** _____

☐ Answer Requested (SASE enclosed).   ☐ No answer needed.

BUYER'S RESPONSE:

SELL-A-GRAM

from a reader of Tony Hyman's *I'll Buy That Too!*

TO: _____

FROM: _____

Phone: ( )

I have the following item:

Remember to include the (1) shape, (2) colors, (3) dimensions, and (4) all names, dates, and marks. Re-read pages 10-14 and any text or entry notes for selling what you have.

It's condition is:

List all chips, repairs, cracks, dents, fading, scratches, rips, tears, creases, holes, stains, and foxing. Note any missing pages, parts, or paint.

Music Boxes

Mechanical musical instruments cover a side range of music boxes, band organs, monkey organs, coin pianos, etc. Basically they represent any musical instruments that play by themselves. Our specialty is pre-1920, and excludes regular player pianos.

DISC MUSIC BOXES:

Regina 12" disc music box	$600
Regina 12" disc music box, gum vendor	2,000
Regina 15-1/2" disc single comb music box	1,500
Regina 15-1/2" disc double comb music box	2,000
Regina 20-1/2" disc double comb music box	3,000
Regina 27" disc double comb music box with folding top	5,000
Regina 27" disc music box in upright case	8,000
Regina 15-1/2 disc music box, changes 12 discs automatically	12,500
Regina 27" disc music box, changes 12 discs automatically	13,500
Polyphon 15-1/2 disc double comb music box	2,000
Polyphon 19-5/8" disc upright music box	3,500
Polyphon 22-1/4 disc upright music box with bells	6,500
Polyphon 24-1/2 disc upright music box with base cabinet	7,000
Symphonion 19-1/8" upright disc music box	3,000
Symphonion 3-disc upright music box	15,000
Symphonion 3-disc upright music box with clock	20,000
Mira 18-1/2 disc music box, table model	4,000
Mira 18-1/2" disc music box, console floor model	5,500
Lochmann 24-1/2 disc music box with bells	9,000
Capital Cuff music box, 4-1/2" cuff	1,500

CYLINDER MUSIC BOXES:

Nicole Freres 13" x 2-1/2" cylinder keywind music box	$800
Nicole Freres 13" x 4" cylinder keywind music box	3,000
Nicole Freres 17-1/2" x 4" cylinder keywind music box	6,000
Mermod Freres 14" cylinder music box	1,000
Mermod Freres 14" cylinder music box with bells	1,250
Mermod Freres 14" cylinder music box, four cylinders	2,500
Mermod Freres 20-1/2" cylinder music box, five cylinders, table	7,500
Mermod Freres 24-1/2" cylinder music box, six cylinders, table	15,000
Paillard 18" cylinder music box	1,500
Paillard 18" cylinder music box, four cylinders	3,500
Paillard 18" cylinder music box, five cylinders, table	5,000
Snuff box cylinder music box, before 1840	250
"Pleriodinique" style music box, multiple cylinders	10,000
Cylinder music box with six cylinders mounted on "carousel"	15,000

MECHANICAL BIRDS:

Early bird cage, single bird, separate key winds from side	$450
Early bird cage, two birds, separate key winds from side	750
Early bird cage, three birds, separate key winds from side	1,000
Twentieth century bird box with singing bird	300
Early fusee wind box with singing bird	1,000
Automaton with clock and five mechanical birds under glass dome	2,000

BAND ORGANS:

Wurlitzer style 125 band organ, brass trumpets, playing	$12,000
Wurlitzer style 150 band organ, brass trumpets, playing	16,000
Wurlitzer style 153 band organ, playing	20,000

ORCHESTRIONS:

Mills Violano Virtuoso automatic violin, good condition	$8,000
Hupfeld Phonolit, three violins, automatic with piano	100,000
Seeburg L 44-note cabinet style piano, working	3,000
Seeburg Eagle style piano with pipes	5,000
Wurlitzer style H orchestrion, carved female posts	55,000
Large Weber orchestrion	15,000
Large Welte orchestrion with "sunburst" metal trumpets	30,000

MONKEY ORGAN:

25-key Molinari with 38 pipes	$2000
42-key Bacigalupo with 90 pipes	5,000
38-key Frati with 80 pipes and brass trumpets in front	6,500

Prices Paid by: Martin Roenigk, Mechantiques
26 Barton Hill
East Hampton, CT 06424

(203) 267-8682
FAX (203) 267-1120

Because these instruments vary so widely, and so many different models were made, we will need several good photographs from different angles.

Cookie Jars

The jars I collect date from the 1930's through 1960's, with a few of later dates. Their values range from $35 to $250. The prices I'm quoting you refer to jars in "perfect" condition for their age. This means absolutely no chips, cracks or flakes. Crazing of the glaze is tolerated to a certain extent as is wear in the paint on some jars.

In parentheses, I've given the maker or the identifying mark you can look for. Please send a snapshot of your jar with SASE for reply.

Astronauts (McCoy)	$150
Cheerleaders (Amer. Bisque)	100
Chef (Amer. Bisque)	75
Chef (Pearl China)	250
Circus Horse (Brush)	200
Coalby Cat (McCoy)	150
Cow, purple (Brush)	125
Cow/Moon (Robinson Ransbottom)	100
Davy Crockett (Amer. Bisque)	100
Dutch Boy (Robinson Ransbottom)	75
Elephant/ice cream cone (Brush)	150
Flintstones (Amer. Bisque)	200
Globe (McCoy)	75
Hippo & monkey (Brush)	200
Honey Bear (Amer. Bisque)	100
Humpty Dumpty (Brush)	75
Jack O'Lantern (McCoy)	150
Jocko (Robinson Ransbottom)	100
Kittens on Yarn	50
Leprechaun (McCoy)	400
Little Audrey (Amer. Bisque)	250
Majorette (Amer. Busque)	100
Majorette (Regal)	100
Mammy (Pearl China)	250
Old Clock (Brush)	100
Out of this World (Amer. Bisque)	100
Peek a Boo (Regal)	500
Peter Pan (Brish)	500
Pinocchio (Metlox)	100
Popeye (Amer. Bisque)	300
Rose (Metlox)	100
School Girl (Amer. Bisque)	100
Snowman (Robinson Ransbotom)	150
Soldier (Cardinal)	75
Soldier on Drum (Shawnee)	100
Swee' Pea (Amer. Bisque)	500
Teepee (McCoy)	100
Toaster (Vandor)	75
Umbrella Kids (Amer. Bisque)	100
Whale (Robinson Ransbottom)	300
Witch (Abington)	200

"Coalby Cat" in excellent condition, $150

Prices Paid by: Kier Linn
2591 Military Ave.
Los Angeles, CA 90064

(310) 477-5229

Stoneware & Crocks

Birds $200 - $5,000

There has been stoneware, redware and related items made since the early 1700's. These things were made to be used on an everyday purpose. They were used for the daily table for eating off, for drinking out of, for making butter, for holding whiskey, wine, apple cider. You name it, it had a good use. These items are collectors items today for their form, their decorations, their overall appeal. These were made from all locations all over the country, especially here in N. J, N.Y. where they found great clay for the making of these items. The money is in the decoration. The greater the blue, the better the money. condition means a lot. Cracks, chips, etc. hurt the value. Pieces with flowers, birds, are common. We pay a premium for stoneware with animals, ships, peacocks, houses and other odd decorations. Remember, the greater the blue the more money we pay. Look for pieces that are stamped with the maker's mark. We also want Southern pottery, decorated redware, etc. Any jug, crock, pitcher, churn, canning jars, etc. with strange decorations, we will pay top dollar.

For pieces with these decorations, we will pay the following
(These are all blue decorated done in a blue cobalt):

Deer	$1,500-6000
People	2,500-10,000+
Trees & houses	1,000-3,000+
Peacocks	2,500-5,000+
Birds	200-5000+
Florals	100-1,000+
Man in the moon	1,000-2,500+
Lions	3-10,000+
Horses	2-5,000+
Trains	10,000+
Decorated Inkwells	500-2,500+
Ships	1,500-4000+
Flasks	300-3,500
Flags	1,000-10,000+

People $2,500 - $10,000+

Look for names like BENNINGTON VT, COWDEN & WILCOX PA, T. HARRINGTON LYONS NY, FULPER BROTHERS FLEMMINGTON, NJ, FT. EDWARD POTTER CO. NY plus any stamped pottery from any southern and mid western potteries.

Also any signed NJ, NY, Rockingham pitchers, etc. paying from $250 to $5,000.

Decorated redware plates, bowls, pitchers–these items are colored in a yellow, green slip. They range from simple yellow decorations to names on them and the best ones are multi-colored with different colors.

Paying top dollar for plates with scenes, animals, etc.

Any plate, bowl with horses, people, dates – $1,000 to $15,000

The better ones are usually Pennsylvania or southern. Some are done in German writing from the Pennsylvania Dutch. Again, condition is very important.

Deer $1,500-$6,000

Plates $1,000 - $15,000

Prices Paid by: R.C. Hume
P.O. Box 281
Bay Head, NJ 08742
Send good photos and list condition for true estimates.

Glass Paperweights

Top quality glass paperweights and related items have been made in three distinct periods since the early 1840's. A good paperweight is made of clear glass, with a colored design suspended inside. The basic types are:

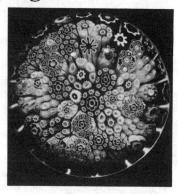

Millefiori: has thin "Christmas candy" like slices of colored glass, which may be arranged in a variety of different designs, or simply packed closely together.

Lampwork: realistic or stylized representations of flowers, reptiles, insects or fruit, etc., are surrounded by clear glass.

Sulphides: (cameo incrustations) a white "ceramic", or colored silver or gold foil depiction of a famous person, historical or Biblical event, or military insignia.

The shape of a good weight is usually a slightly flattened sphere with a flat (actually slightly concave) base. The surface may be cut with "windows". Rarer weights sometimes are covered with one or two layers of colored glass, cut with "windows", through which the design is visible.

VALUE: The value of a glass paperweight is determined by a number of factors, the most important being; artist or factory, rarity, design, beauty, craftsmanship and condition.

CLASSIC PERIOD 1845-1870

Made in France, England, the United States, Bohemia and Venice. Rare exceptional weights can be worth as much as $50,000., with an average weight bringing around $1,000. Most antique weights are not signed or dated. Those that are will contain a tiny initial B, C, J, IGW, SL etc. inside the design, with or without a date. Legitimate dates are, 1845, 1846, 1847, 1848, 1849, 1852 (and inverted appearing as 1825), 1853, and 1858. Other nineteenth century dates are fake, most often appearing in Italian weights from the past few decades.

INTERMEDIATE YEARS 1870-1950

Very few good paperweights were made during this period. Those that were, feature three dimensional, realistic lampwork, flowers, fruit, butterflies and reptiles. In the late nineteenth century good weights were made by Mt. Washington Glass Company in the United States, Pantin in France, and an unknown maker most likely in Russia. Another type of weight featuring crimp flowers was made by several individuals in the Millville, NJ area in the early 1900's. The Pantin and Mt. Washington weights are often large, 4" or more in diameter. "Millville" weights have a clear glass foot or pedestal. The "Russian" weights are often flat, rectangular plaques containing flowers or fruit. We will pay up to $2,000 for the best Millville weights, and from $5,000 to $10,000 for good examples from the other makers. Weights from this period are not signed or dated.

Most top quality contemporary weights are signed internally or on the surface with the artists' initials or name. Listed below are the names of the makers we are most interested in purchasing. Prices paid range from $50 to over $5,000 depending on the maker and design.

Ayotte, Rick	Kontes, James	Stankard, Paul
Baccarat	Kontes, Nontas	Tarsitano, Debbie
Banford, Bob	Labino, Dominick	Tarsitano, Delmo
Banford, Bobby	Littleton, Harvey	Trabucco, David & Jon
Banford, Ray	Manson, William	Trabucco, Victor
Buzzini, Chris	Parsley, Johne	Whitefriars
Donofrio, Jim	Perthshire	Whittemore, Francis
Grubb, Randall	Rosenfeld, Ken	Ysart, Paul
"J" Glass	Saint Louis	
Kaziun, Charles	Smith, Gordon	

Paperweight related items wanted

Other glass objects incorporating paperweight decorating techniques in the base or body of the object are also wanted. These objects include: bottles, boxes, candlesticks, cups, doorknobs, goblets, lamps, letter presses, mantel ornaments, marbles, obelisks, perfumes, plates, plaques, snuff mulls and tumblers.

Paperweight literature, auction catalogues and books also wanted.

Magazines with articles about paperweights are worth $1 each. Auction catalogues devoted to glass paperweights are worth from $1-5 each. Books about paperweights are worth from $5-100.

NOT WANTED:

Murano weights (usually have perfectly flat base)	**Advertising weights**	**Weights with large bubbles & swirls of color as part of the design**
Chinese weights (glass often is greasy feeling and appears yellowish, design contains "school bus" yellow)	**Souvenir weights** **Weights with fake dates** (before 1845, or in the 1860's, 70's or 80's	**Colored apples & pears on a clear "cookie" base are acceptable**
	Cute shapes (dogs, cats, etc.)	

Books about paperweights available

Old Glass paperweights of Southern New Jersey	$20
Paperweights of the 19th and 20th Centuries	60
The Jokelson Collection of Antique Cameo Incrustation	60

Available postage paid by sending a check to:
Papier Presse, PO Box 6269, Statesville, NC 28687-6269

Prices Paid by: Paul Dunlop
PO Box 6269
Statesville, NC 28687   (800) 227-1996

Cast Iron Cookware

Griswold is the most popular cast iron cookware collectible, however, there is interest in unusual pieces by other makers. These include: Wagner, Piqua, Favorite, Wapak, G.F. Filley, Martin, etc. I am also interested in coffee roasters, broilers and baking pans even if unmarked. Griswold skillets must be marked with the large logo (about 3˝ dia.) or ERIE. Prices quoted are for black iron. Nickle finish are worth about 25% less.

Pieces must be in good condition, free from cracks, chips, and crusted rust. Light rust and burned grease is OK. Please do not clean them. I prefer to clean them myself!

Griswold skillets #s 3, 6 & 8 are worth $5 unless marked Al Carder, Cliff Cornell, or Victor, in which case they are worth $30-150. A #5 Victor is worth $250.

GRISWOLD

Muffin/Gem/Cornstick Pans

#2800	Wheat or Corn	$1,000
#2700	Wheat or Corn	250
#28	ERIE single Loaf	1,000
#26	ERIE double Loaf	500
#1	Single Vienna Roll	500
#2	Double Vienna Roll	200
#4	(957) Vienna Roll	200
#280	Wheat or Corn	350
#270	Wheat or Corn	150
#50	Hearts Star	500
#100	Hearts Star	250
#19	Golf Ball	250
#9	Golf Ball	85
#240	Turks Head	150
#130	Turks Head	230
#140	Turks Head	100
#13	Turks Head	450
#14	Turks Head	350
#1		100
#3		250
#5		250

Erie No. 28 $1000

Toys - "0" or "00" Size

(may be marked "2" or "4")

Griddle	$100
Dutch Oven	100
Tea Kettle	250
Waffle Iron	1,000
Pup #30	100
Aluminum Toys	50

Skillets (Lg Logo)

#0	
#1	40
#2	1,000
	175

#4	25
#5	10
#7	8
#9	12
#10	25
#11	75
#12	45
#13	350
#14	75
#14 w/bail handle	500
#20	250
All In One (3 sec)	200
Spider Logo "ERIE"	700
Oval Skillet #15	125
Oval Skillet #13	200
Double Skillet (top & btm)	50

Skillet Covers

#3 - #9	$25
#10	35
#11 & 12	50
#13, 14, 20	150

Round Griddles

(20 more for Diamond Logo)

#6	$35
#10	20
#14	25
#16	35
Vapor Briddle	125

Dutch Ovens

#6	$75
#7	35
#10	50
#11	100
#12	150
#13	250

Oval Roasters

(add $25 with trivet)

#3	$350
#5	200
#7	200
#9	350

Waffle Irons

#6	$150
#7	45
Hearts Star #18	90
Hearts Star #19	150
Square #s "0", "00", #1, #2	200

Cake Molds

Santa	$400
Rabbit	175
Lamb	65
Bundt	500

Wagner Wire No. 1 $500

Miscellaneous

5 in 1 Breakfast Skillet	$100
110 Skillet Griddle	50
Double Broiler	150
Coffee Grinder	400
Alum Bread Slicer	200
Dutch Oven Rack (5 tier)	750
Dutch Oven Rack (3 tier)	500
Griddle Rack	200
Skillet Rack	125
Sun Dial	200
Loaf Pan	200
Loaf Pan w/cover	350
Coffee Roaster	400
Wafer Iron w/base	225

WAGNER Ware Gem Pans

#1 Handled Gem Pan	$500
Style "M" 4 section	350
STyle "N" 4 section	350

WAPAK

Indian Head Skillet	$40-250

*Also Wanted – Trade Catalogs which includes Cast Iron Cookware $200+
**I am not interested in #8 Dutch Ovens or #'s 10, 11, 22
      or #273 Muffin or Bread Stick Pans.

Prices Paid by: David G. Smith, "Pan Man"
                     Drawer B
                     Perrysburg, NY 14129   (716) 532-5154

Silverware

Value - General Model
(MOST patterns will fall
into this range)

Stainless   5¢-$1 per piece
Silverplate 5¢-$3 per piece
Sterling $5-$30 per piece

MEDICI
SEA SCULPTURE
KING EDWARD
CAMELLIA
FAIRFAX

TYPES OF SILVERWARE

There are basically 3 types of silverware: 1. Sterling, 2. Silverplate, 3. Stainless. Sterling is usually the most expensive and stainless the least expensive.

VALUATION MODEL

A combination of the following determines value: pattern, maker, condition, size/style/version of piece, and of course, supply and demand. For example, an excellent piece in poor condition can be worth less than an average piece in excellent condition. This rule can be applied to many material objects besides silverware. Dented knife handles, pitted knife blades, monograms, and excessive wear all detract from value.

WISHFUL THINKING

People often "wish" the silverware they have is sterling. Unfortunately, worth and wish are two difference things. Generally, if it is sterling it will be marked "sterling" or 925/1000." If you bother to make the best, you mark it as such.

Generally, if it is silverplate it has the look of sterling but not the marks of sterling. Some common marks on silverplate are [(any word) and "plate"], "Wm Rogers," "1847 Rogers Bros," and "Holmes & Edwards."

Since silverplate has silver only on the surface, excessive use may cause the silver to wear through to the base metal. Worn silverplate is worth considerably less.

Generally, if it is stainless it will have the look of stainless and be marked "stainless," "18/8" or only with the manufacturer's name. Restaurant stainless has virtually no value.

MidweSterling buys and sells all silverware and holloware. MidweSterling also offers a repair service including knife reblading and disposal repair.

Prices Paid by:	MidweSterling	(816) 454-1990
	4311 NE Vivion, Dept. HY	FAX (816) 454-1605
	Kansas City, MO 64119-2890	Closed Wednesday & Sunday

Banks • Toys • Clocks

STILL BANKS

Hippo	$1,000-2,500
Rhino	250-500
Painted Buildings	100-1,000

CAST IRON, PAINTED TIN

Small cast iron figures	$100-1,000
Boston State House	750-1,500
Palace	750-2,250
Old South Church	750-2,000
Eagle with shield	500-900
Man who looks like a frog	500-2,000
No repro banks desired.	

MECHANICAL BANKS

Acrobat	$500-4,000
Atlas bank	500-2,500
Bad accident	500-2,000
Baby elephant	500-2,000
Bill E. Gien	100-300
Bowling alley bank	1,000-10,000
Boy in birds nest	500-7,000
Bread winners bank	1,000-12,000
Bull dog	500-20,000
Butting buffalo	500-2,000
Calamity	1,000-7,000
Cat and mouse	500-2,000
Chimpanzee	500-2,500
Chinaman	500-2,000
Clown banks depend on type	500-5,000
Confectionery	500-5000
Cupola	500-4,000
Baseball (Darktown battery)	500-4,000
Watermelon with man	500-4,000
Dentist	500-2,000
Ding dong bell	250-1,500
Elephants (type)	250-4,000
Freedmans	10,000-50,000
Giant	200-3,500
Girl skipping rope	5,000-25,000
Hen & chicken	500-1,500
Home bank	500-1,500
Horse race	500-4,500
Jonah & whale	500-3,000
Little Mae	500-3,000
Magician	500-2,500
Mommy & child	500-4,750
Merry-go-round	2,500-12,500
Mason	500-4,000
Milking cow	500-6,000
Mikado	500-12,500
Monkey (type)	250-3,000
North Pole	250-3,000
Organ grinder (type)	250-4,500
Panorama bank	500-7,000
Paddy	250-5,000
Picture gallery	1,250-12,500
Presto bank	100-2,000
Pug dog	100-5,000
Roller skating	1,000-10,000
Santa Claus	500-4,000
Dog & tree	500-2,500
Man shooting bird	1,000-5,000
Man stealing chickens	1,000-5,000
Turtle	500-1,500
Uncle Sam	500-5,000

Foot Ball Bank
Circa 1905.
$7,500

Home Bank
Circa 1880
$2,000

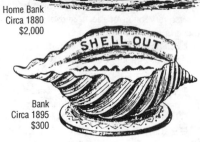

Bank
Circa 1895
$300

The Chinaman Bank
Circa 1885
$4,000

No J.N. wanted.

I will buy **broken banks** for parts. Call for other undescribed banks and tell me about bank condition, etc.!

OTHER BANK ITEMS

I will buy **boxes, catalogues and trade cards** of banks still and mechanical.

These are what the banks were packed in:

Wooden packaging boxes	$200-2,000
Cardboard packaging boxes	100-1,000

PHOTOS of children and banks   100-1,000

MULTICOLORED ADVERTISING CARDS

(no repros wanted)

Picture gallery bank	$500-2,500
Watch dog safe bank	500-2,500
Trick dog bank	400-2,000
Baseball bank	400-1,600
One color advertising flyers	25-100

CATALOGUES OF BANK COMPANIES

J & E Stevens, Cromwell, CT	$100-500
Kyser & Rex, Phila., PA	100-500
Shepard Hardware, Buffalo, NY	100-500

MOBY DICK (actual book)

1st edition, U.S.	$4,500-9,000
1st edition, British	10,000
1930 edition, Chicago lakeside with case	750-1,250

SCRIMSHAW

Whale scrimshaw only!
Wanted 1820-1900

Whale tooth scrimshaw	$250-10,000
Boxes with inlay	250-2,000
Swifts	250-8,000
Kitchen implements	250-7,500

Must be old and interesting. Erotic scrimshaw desired. (Only American. No netsuke.) No modern. Pre-1900 desired.

CLOCKS (Only old clocks wanted)

Old 1860-1880 cast iron, painted.
Blinking Eye Clocks

Elf	$500-2,000
Dog	500-1,500
Man on keg of beer	500-2,000
Dancing black lady	500-2,000
Man playing banjo	500-1,500
Lion	500-1,250

DOUBLE DIAL CLOCK – tells time,

day, date, month, day of week

Ithaca, Ingraham, Seth Thomas	$500-5,000
Early American banjo clocks	500-2,500

CATALOGUES OF DOUBLE DIAL CLOCKS

Early clock catalogues $100-400

No repros, fakes, or electric. Only American pre-1910.

SIGN SPECTACLES.

$750

DENTISTS' SIGNS.

$750

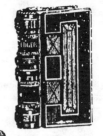

BOOK SIGNS.

$750

Topsey. One Day Clock
Circa 1870. $1,500

Eight-day Timepiece
Circa 1870, $1,500

Office Calendar
Circa 1875, $2,000

SAFES

I like small safes, less than 30" high with lots of pinstripping and a small painted picture in vignette.

Small safes $250-1250

Depends on conditions, pinstripping, color (white, burgundy a premium color) and picture. Must be from the 1870-1920 period.

Toy cast iron safe banks
Painted	$100-300
Nickel	100-300

Toy and real safe catalogues bought $50-200

Do not desire large safes larger than 30", especially want a small, round headed safe.

LEVER SEALS

From the 1860-1920 era. Especially want cast iron figural ones.

Rams head	$50-150
Eagle	50-250
Toad	50-250
Salamander	50-250
etc.	

Must be ornate, no rust and in working order.

Plain seals not wanted except if very ornate or unusual subject – KKK, Coca Cola, whore house, toy company, etc.

EARLY AMERICAN TIN TOYS – Pull & Wind Up,
1860-1900 (Clockworks)

Monitor (battleship)	$1,000-4,000
Omnibus (larger the better)	2,000-10,000
Fire Toys	
Wagon, Ladder	1,000-4,000
Pumper	1,000-4,000
Chariot with bank	1,000-4,000
Boats	
Riverboat, paddle boat	1,000-6,000
Monitor	1,000-4,000
Animals	100-600
Animals in hoops	100-750
People	
Black man playing banjo	1,000-10,000
Black man playing bones	1,000-10,000
Black man playing Tambourine	1,000,10,000
Horsedrawn	200-2,000
Buck board	500-1,500
Clockwork fabric covered	
Toys	1,000-5,000
Tin building banks	
The more ornate the better	100-1,000

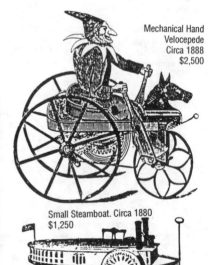

Mechanical Hand
Velocepede
Circa 1888
$2,500

Small Steamboat. Circa 1880
$1,250

Harris Bank. Circa 1900. $475

Hose Carriage
Circa 1880. $2,750

Prices Paid by:	G. ("Dr. Z") Zemenick
	1350 Kirts, Suite 160
	Troy, MI 48084
	8 am-9 pm EST: (810) 642-8129

Model Kits & Toys

MODEL KITS

Note: must be unused in near mint box to qualify for listed prices

Godzilla's Go-cart	$2,000
King Kong's Thronester	2,000
Lost in Space #420	750
Gigantic Frankenstein	750
King Kong (original shrink wrap) #468	500
Godzilla (original shrink wrap) #469	500
Banana Splits buggy	200
Munsters (original shrink wrap)	700
T-Rex	100
Ghidrah	150
Rodan	150
Monster scenes Dr. Jekyll/Mr. Hyde	150
Monster scenes Dracula	150
Frankenstein #423 (original shrink wrap)	400
Mad Doctor, Mad Dentist, Mad Barber	500 ea.
Weird-Ohs customizing kit	200
Robbin Hood Fink	150
Tweedy Pie with Boss Fink	150
Dr. Seuss related	90 ea.
Space Station #1805, Revell	250

1930s - 1950s TOYS

1930s Three Pigs and Big Bad Wolf, wristwatch, boxed	1,000
1930s Three Pigs and Big Bad Wolf alarm clock, boxed	1,250
Mickey Mouse waddle book, unpunched	2,500
Wizard of Oz waddle book, unpunched	2,000
1930 Mickey Mouse book, Bibo & Lang, complete	1,500
Betty Boop pocket watch, boxed	1,800
1930s Betty Boop candy bar box	500
Donald Duck pocket watch, boxed	900
Mickey Mouse pulled by Horace Horsecollar, celluloid	5,000
Mickey and Minnie on motorcycle, Germany tin	7,000
Mickey Dancing with Donald, celluloid	1,000

1960s TOYS

Gunsmoke Marx playset, boxed	$1,250
Johnny Ringo Marx playset, boxed	800
Untouchables Marx playset, boxed	1,100
Hot wheels sky show, 1970, boxed	300
GI Joe green beret, boxed	950
GI Joe aquanaut #7910, boxed	900
GI Joe negro adventurer #7905, boxed	650
GI Joe staff car, boxed	600
GI Joe crash crew fire truck, boxed	850
GI Joe desert patrol attack jeep, boxed	900
Voyage to the Bottom of the Sea gun set, boxed	500
Batman Ideal utility belt, boxed	1,000
Green hornet dashboard, boxed	650
Beatles yellow sub cereal box	250
Frankenstein Marx robot, boxed	750
Jetsons Rosie the Robot windup, boxed	700
Lost in Space Roto-Jet gun, boxed	1,200
Ideal 12" Batgirl, Wonder Woman, Mera, Supergirl, boxed	500 ea.
Creature, Mummy, Wolfman, etc. vacuform wall plaques	200 ea.
Famous Monsters photo printing set, boxed	300
Creature, Mummy, Phantom board games	250 ea.
Cragstan Mr. Atomic Robot, boxed	6,500
Capt. Action Green Hornet or Spiderman outfits, boxed	1,000 ea.
Capt. Action, Dr. Evil's lab set, boxed	900
Mattel Matt Mason scorpio alien, boxed	500
Hasbro GI nurse, boxed	1,000
Johnny Quest P-F Flyers shoe sign	500
Capt. Action Kool Pops box	350
Ideal Batman playset, boxed	650
Ideal justice league playset, boxed	900

Always interested in rare and quality items in these categories. Special interest in original packaging and store signs and displays related. Condition is critical. Some of the listed items in bad shape may not be of any interest at all.

Prices Paid by: David Welch
2308 Clay St., P.O. Box 714
Murphysboro, IL 62966

(618) 687-2282
FAX (618) 684-2243

Toy Guns - Cap & BB

Red Ryder BB Guns
Red Ryder BB guns marked No. 111 $100
Model 40, with Copper Plated
barrel Bands and iron cocking lever.

Substantial rewards paid for most older air rifles with iron cocking levers. (Use a magnet) Also for related Red Ryder collectibles.

Old BB Guns & Cap Pistols
Daisy BB guns with wire stocks	$250
BB guns marked Bulls Eye	200
Cast iron BB guns marked Heilprin	200
BB guns marked Cycloid	175
BB guns marked Cyclone	175
BB guns marked Atlas	175
BB guns marked Matchless	175
BB guns marked Magic	175
BB guns marked Bojou	175
BB guns marked General Custer	175
BB guns marked Dewey or Crescent	150
BB guns marked Globe	150
BB guns marked Warrior	150
BB guns marked Hexagon	150
BB guns marked Remington	150
BB guns marked Columbia	125
BB guns marked Sterling	125
BB guns marked American Tool Works	125
BB guns marked American Dart Rifle	100
BB guns marked Wyandotte	75
BB guns marked Upton	50

Cap Pistols
Will pay for the following cast iron cap pistols in good to mint condition. Higher rewards for pieces in the orginal box.
Cap pistols marked Roy Rogers	$200
Cap pistols marked Long Tom	150
Cap pistols marked American	150
Cap pistols marked Big Horn	75
Cap pistols marked Gene Autry	50
Cap pistols marked Lone Ranger	50

Substantial rewards for other Cast Iron, Western Style Cap Pistols.

Cast Iron cap pistols by Kilgore. Top left: "Long Tom," $150. Top Right: "Roy Rogers," $200. Center: "American," $150. Bottom Left & Right: "Big Horn." $75. Premium prices for guns in mint condition. Pay more for guns in original box.

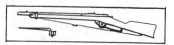

Daisy Military Guns. No. 40 & No. 140. Both came with sling & No. 40 came with detachable bayonet. $50-100 for BB gun. $50-100 for bayonet.

Early Daisys. All were originally nickel plated. Most are break action & have cast metal frame or trigger guards. A few have a top cocking lever. Some have wire stocks. $75-400 depending on model and condition.

Daisy Red Ryder, No. 111 model 40. With cast iron cocking levers. $40-75. Premium prices for guns with copper plated barrel bands and/or color lithographed original boxes.

"1000 Shot Daisy" or "500 Shot Daisy." Have 1901 & 1904 patent numbers. No model numbers. $75-150 depending on condition. Guns are nickel plated.

Daisy Buzz Barton guns. $50-75 for blued guns with oval stock label or brand. $75-150 for nickel plated guns with star stock brand. Guns must have rear sight tube & elevated front sight as shown to command full price.

Trombone pumps by Daisy or King. Marked "King No. 5 Pump Gun," "Daisy No. 105 Junior Pump Gun," "Daisy No. 107 Buck Jones" or "Ranger Pump Gun, Sear Roebuck & Co." $75-150 depending on model and condition. Daisy No. 25's are not included in this group.

Prices Paid by:	Jim Buskirk
	175 Cornell Street
	Windsor, CA 95492
	(707) 837-9949

Toys & Motorcycles

Listed below are prices I will pay.
Toys in original boxes will bring more.

Buddy-L-Toys

Fire truck	$100-500
Fire pumper	100-500
Fire aerial ladder	200-600
Fire water tower	200-700
Fliver coupe	300-600
Ford express truck	500-1,000
Oil truck	300-800
Ice truck	300-600

Matchbox toys, in original boxes only	10-50
Dinkey toys	10-50
Disney toys	100-5,000
Marx toys	50-1,000
Fisher Price, Elsie's Dairy Truck	100-300
Erector sets, wood boxes only, #10 set	1,000-2,000
Japanese toys	100-2,000
German toys	100-5,000
Tootsie toys	10-500

Toy Robots $100-5,000

Wolverine	
Honeymooners bus	$100-400
Merry-go-round	100-200
Zilotone	100-300
Wyandote	
Circus truck	100-300
Ambulance	50-100

$100-2,000 & Up

$50-500

Lincoln (Canada)– Coke truck	$100-500
Metal craft	
Coke truck	200-500
Heinz truck	100-400

$100-1,000 & Up

Buying Motorcycles and Motorcycle Items

Indian motorcycles	$1,000-5,000
Harley Davidson	1,000-5,000
Cycle signs, awards, fobs, posters, pins, paper items	100-5,000
Cushman Motorscooters, Whizzer and Mustang Motorbikes	100-1,000

$200-500 & Up

Prices Paid by: Chris Savino
P.O. Box 419
Breesport, NY 14816   (609) 739-3106

Toy Trains & Related Items

Lionel, American Flyer, Ives, Dorfan, Voltamp, Carlisle & Finch, Marx and Hafner Overland Flyer are the best known American brands of toy trains. Hundreds of such brands exist, most of which are to some degree collectible.

Original condition is the most important factor in determining value. A toy train set that may be old but is still unused, pristine and "mint" in the original box will command the highest price. Heavily-used, dented, scratched, rusted or repainted toy trains have only minimal or parts value. A toy train is like buying a new car in that, once you drive it out of the showroom, it loses a lot of its value. A like-new toy train may lose one third of its value the first time it is played with.

The following represents prices that will be paid for mint in-the-original-box toy trains. Similar toy trains that are used and not mint and not in the original boxes will bring much lower prices.

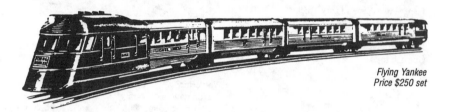

Flying Yankee
Price $250 set

LIONEL TRAINS

State set, 4 car brown, c. 1930's	$6,000
State set, 3 or 4 car green, c. 1930's	4,000
Blue Comet set, c. 1930's	3,000
Hiawatha #250E passenger set, c. 1930's	2,000
Railchief Passenger set with #700E (5344) Hudson	5,000
"Baby" Blue Comet "0" gauge set, #263E, c. 1930's	1,500
Mickey Mouse circus set, c. 1930's	1,500
Mickey Mouse freight set, c. 1930's	1,000
Disney handcars, c. 1930's, featuring Mickey Mouse, Minnie Mouse, Santa Claus, Donald Duck, Pluto & Peter Rabbit	500
Hudson locomotive #5344 (700E)	2,000
Hudson locomotive #5344 (700K) in kit form	4,000
Hudson locomotive #763, grey	1,000
Hudson locomotive #773, c. 1950	1,000
GG1, bi-polar electric engines #2330, 2332, 2340, 2360	500-1,000
Blue Streak #265E set, c. 1039's	500
Red Comet #264 set, c. 1930's	250
General #1872 deluxe set	400
C & O diesel #624	200
Seaboard #6250 diesel	200
Shell Oil tank car #515	500
Automobile loader #6414 with 4 green cars	175
Sunoco oil tanker #2555	100
Texas Special #2245 AB locomotive pair	400
B & O #2368 F3 locomotive pair	1,500
Rio Grande #2379 F3 AB locomotive pair	1,000
Sante Fe #2333 AA locomotive pair	1,000
Milwaukee Road #2378 AB locomotive pair	2,000
Southern #2356 ABA locomotive trio	2,000
Jersey Central #2341 FM locomotive	1,500
Virginian #2341 FM locomotive	1,000
Union Pacific #2023 Yellow & Grey set	1,500
Flying Yankee #616 4 piece streamliner set	250
Apple Green 4 car 408E set	400
Work Train with #1835 engine & 4 cars	1,000
Locomotive #'s 400E, 392E or 1835E	400+
Switcher locomotive #8976 in full-scale set, c. 1930's	2,000
Switcher #8976 semi-scale locomotive only	300
Refrigerated box car #214R	250
Union Pacific streamliner set #752W, silver or yellow & brown	300+
Large metal building & bridges	100-1,000

AMERICAN FLYER

"S" gauge Northern Pacific passenger set	$1,000
"S" gauge Missouri Pacific passenger set	1,000
Mayflower wide gauge passenger set	5,000
President's Special wide gauge passenger set	3,000
Rocky Mountain wide gauge freight set	2,500
"0" gauge Ambassador passenger set	300
"0" gauge Golden State or Jeffersonian passenger set	250
"0" gauge Potomac passenger set	200
"0" gauge wind-up set	50-250
"0" gauge 3/16" scale sets with 806 or 573 engines	250-500
"0" gauge Burlington Zephyr cast aluminum sets	200+
"0" gauge streamlined passenger sets with cars in blue, chrome, red, yellow & brown, or green (12 wheeled cars better than 8 wheeled cars)	400-800

IVES

Standard gauge white passenger set	$5,000+
Prosperity Special sets	5,000+
Standard gauge lithographed freight sets	1,000+
"0" gauge lithographed freight sets	500+
"0" gauge, any other complete set	250+
Accessories, buildings, etc	25-250

MARX, MARLINES, LINEMAR

Mickey Mouse set	$250
Super Circus set	500
Streamlined passenger sets	50-100
Most other sets	10-30

HAFNER "OVERLAND FLYER" WIND-UP TRAIN SETS

c. 1914-1935 sets	$100+
c. 1935-1950 sets	50+
c. 1951+ sets made by Wyandotte	25

FOREIGN MADE TOY TRAINS, "0" GAUGE OR LARGER

Maerklin "Crocodile" locomotive	$2,000+
Bing, Karl Bub (KBN), Maerklin sets	100-1,000+
Hornby, British or French sets	100+
Assessories, buildings, etc.	10-500

DORFAN

Standard gauge passenger sets	$500-1,000
Standard gauge lithographed freight sets	500-1,000
"0" gauge lithographed freight sets	300-500
"0" gauge passenger sets	200-350
Accessories, buildings, etc.	25-250

Lionel Hudson 700E
Price $2,000

In communicating about your toy trains, please include complete piece descriptions including serial numbers, color, condition, etc. and/or send along some good photographs.

I am also authorized to accept tax deductible donations of toy trains on behalf of the Toy Train Historical Foundation, a registered charity, for display at the California State Railroad Museum. Call for more information.

Prices Paid by:	Dr. Hilly Lazarus
	14547 Titus St., Suite 207
	Panorama City, CA 91402
	Evening & Weekend phone: (818) 762-3652

Barbie Dolls

BARBIE & FAMILY

NUMBER ONE: Brunette, retouched red lips, near mint in box with swimsuit, shoes, glasses, hoop earrings, number one booklet and box.   1200-1500
NUMBER TWO: Blonde, sumptuous red lips, long thick hair, pinky pink skin, beautiful complexion, mint in box with everything. 1500-2000
NUMBER THREE: Blonde, blue eye liner, red lips, otherwise excellent condition   150-200
NUMBER THREE: Blonde, blue eye liner, all original in her black and white swimsuit, excellent condition.   125-150
NUMBER FOUR: Brunette, red lips & long hair. Swimsuit, pretty face, excellent condition.   100-150
NUMBER FIVE: Redhead, red lips, gorgeous face, Swimsuit, excellent condition.   75-100
NUMBER FIVE: Blonde, gorgeous aqua eyes, red lips, nude, smashing, excellent condition.   50-75
NUMBER SIX: Ash blonde, coral lips, attractively pretty face and body, excellent condition.   50-75
BUBBLE CUT: Black hair, red lips, mint in box, complete   150-175
BUBBLE CUT: Black hair, red lips, nude, near mint.   30-50
BUBBLE CUT: Red hair, red lips, nude, beautiful face, full hair, excellent condition.   30-50
BUBBLE CUT: Redhead, large watermelon lips, nude, lovely doll, excellent condition.   40-50
BUBBLE CUT: Rare! Brownette color, red lips, black and white swimsuit. mint.   200-250
SWIRL: Blonde, pale orange lips, mint in box with everything (even cheek blush).   200-250
SWIRL: Blonde, retouched coral lips, nude, excellent condition.   50-75
FASHION QUEEN: Blue band, gold and white striped swimsuit, wig stand and 3 wigs, no turban, excellent condition.   95
MISS BARBIE: 23 wigs with wig stand, swimsuit, hat, orange band, tiny melt mark, otherwise mint.   150-175
BENDABLE LEG AMERICAN GIRL: Redhead, pale orange lips, never removed from box.   400
BENDABLE LEG AMERICAN GIRL: redhead, pale orange lips with the really curly hair at the side, mint in box.   350
BENDABLE LEG AMERICAN GIRL: blonde hair, dark orange lips, fabulous mint in box   400
SIDE PART: Doll with black silver hair and original head band, original thread still in hair; color magic face with deep red lips and rosy cheeks and gorgeous eye shadow. Original mint swimsuit, rare   1500
BENDABLE LEG AMERICAN GIRL: Pale blonde, cantaloupe lips, nude, near mint.   200-250
BENDABLE LEG AMERICAN GIRL: Brunette, red lips, slight hair cut, otherwise excellent condition. 100-125
BENDABLE LEG AMERICAN GIRL: Long golden cinnamon hair, coral lips, original swimsuit, near mint   200-300
COLOR MAGIC: Lemon blonde, original hair band and barrette, swimsuit & shoes, deep geranium lavish lips, mint   200-250
HAIR FAIR: Brunette head on standard body, long lashes, rosy cheeks, excellent condition near mint   30-40
HAIR FAIR: Blonde on standard body, excellent condition   20-30
TWIST AND TURN: Platinum, 1967, original top and bottom, no belt, original bow, near mint/mint   50-60
TALKING BARBIE: Dark, dark brunette, 1969, original swimsuit in original box, mint in box. 75-100
LIVING BARBIE: Red hair, with the hard to find centered eyes, long eye lashes. In polka dot swim suit.   30-40
NEW BARBIE WITH GROWIN' PRETTY HAIR: Never removed from box but her box is shop worn   60-80
MONTGOMERY WARDS BARBIE: Mint in box with wrist tag. This is the brown cardboard Ward's box.   250-350
QUICK CURL BARBIE: Original dress, brush, comb and curler, mint   10
DELUXE QUICK CURL BARBIE: Original outfit & shawl, mint   10

STRAIGHT LEG MIDGE: Redhead or brunette, with wrist tag & original liner, never removed from box, mint   95
STRAIGHT LEG MIDGE: Blonde, mint in box with original swimsuit, booklet & shoes, replaced liner   50-60
BENDABLE LEG MIDGE: Blonde, original swimsuit and hair band, near mint   100-125
NEW TALKING STACEY: Red hair, mint in box with reattached wrist tag and 2-piece striped swim suit, mint in box   75-100
TALKING STACEY: Long red hair, in cardboard and celloed box, 2-piece striped swimsuit, never removed from box.   150-175

1976
BEAUTIFUL BRIDE: European version, box worn.   30-40
BEAUTIFUL BRIDE: Made in Korea, box worn.   30-40

1974
GOLD MEDAL KEN SKIER   50

1970
THE SUN SET MALIBU KEN   25

Barbie Older Fashions - Never Removed From Box
COMMUTER SET: With #1 booklet   500
RED FLARE   40-50
DINNER AT 8   40-80
WINTER HOLIDAY   40-60
BUSY GAL   250
AMERICAN AIRLINE STEWARDESS   50-75
OPEN ROAD   90
SINGING IN THE SHOWER   50-60
BALLERINA   75-90
JUNIOR DESIGNER   100-150
SKATER'S WALTZ   100-125
MATINEE FASHION: With spikes   200-225
GOLD 'N GLAMOUR: With spikes   400-500

Barbie Older Fashions – No Boxes
IT'S COLD OUTSIDE: In brown, complete, near mint, in red, complete and mint.   20-25
BARBIE IN JAPAN: complete with booklet   100-150
CINDERELLA: Complete, near mint with booklet   100-110
ARABIAN NIGHTS: No booklet, otherwise complete and mint.   50-75
LITTLE RED RIDING HOOD: No booklet, otherwise complete and near mint/mint   100-125
CANDY STRIPER VOLUNTEER: Complete, near mint/mint   125-150
GOLDEN GIRL: Complete and near mint.   20-25
GARDEN PARTY: Complete, excellent condition, near mint.   15-20
AFTER FIVE: Complete and excellent condition   15-20
SORORITY MEETING: Complete, near mint.   25-30

Barbie Glamour Group:
Very rare Braniff serving dress, near mint/mint   50-75
Very rare Braniff boarding outfit, no helmet, otherwise complete, near mint/mint   125-175
Boots, mint   30-50

Barbie Pack - Mint on Card
BARBIE DRESS MAKERS   10
SHOE WARDROBE: page 78 Eames   70
PERFECT BEGINNINGS: Hot pink flowered panties & bra with sheer hot pink ruffled half slip, talc &pink puff 25
WHITE & BLACK PRINT BLOUSE: With red purse   10
PINK SATIN BOLERO JACKET AND HAT   25
WHITE SATIN LONG SKIRT: With silver glitter heels   35
FASHION FEET   30

Beatles Memorabilia

Beatles items produced during the group's existence, 1960-1970, are of most interest to collectors. Items produced after 1970 are of little value and interest. Prices quoted are from items in complete, clean condition. Anything considered, examples of key items below.

Toys, games & crafts

Rubber ball	$150
Colorforms	250
5" rubber/plastic dolls	200/set
8" bobbin head dolls	240/set
14" bobbin head dolls	2,000/set
Flip Your Wig game	60
Halloween costumes (boxed)	250
Megaphone	275
Model kits (unbuilt)	150
Paint by number kits	200
Skateboard	1,000

These are just a few of the many items produced bearing the likeness of the greatest group of all time, the Beatles!

Musical Instruments

Banjo & bongos	$500 ea.
Drum	600
Guitars (toy)	100-500 ea.
Harmonica in box	75

Yellow Submarine items

Alarm clock	$300
Banks	150 ea.
Dimensionals	100 ea.
Goebel figurines	500 ea.
Halloween costumes	200
Clothes hangers	50 ea.
Lunch box	150
Puzzles	25-50 ea.
Wristwatch	500

Miscellaneous Items

Record player	$1,000
Concert tickets & stubs	40-150
Clothing & accessories	20-200
Jewelry	30-50
Pennants & posters	20-50
Glasses, dishes, etc.	50-100
School supplies	20-200
Promotional posters & displays	100-1,500
Gum cards, gum card wrappers & boxes	50¢-100

Many other items are wanted. Autographs with good documentation considered. Promotional items of any type are usually of good value, especially records. Picture sleeves for 45's are quite collectible.

Items not wanted include

newspaper clippings
magazines not wholly on the Beatles
photos unless unique
reproductions
solo Beatle items

Prices Paid by: Jeff Augsburger
507 Normal Avenue
Normal, IL 61671

(309) 452-9376
FAX (309) 663-7545

Sellers should provide description of items, include condition, color, identifying marks. Photos are helpful and will be returned. Please include SASE and phone number. Serious collector for over 20 years!

Pop Culture & Nostalgia

Ted Hake established Hake's America in 1967 and today the firm is America's leading mail and telephone bid auction house specializing in nostalgia and popular culture collectibles. Each year Hake's buys and sells 20,000 one of a kind collectibles. Hundreds of thousands of dollars are spent annually to purchase material in over 100 different categories to supply the thousands of worldwide customers who subscribe to five annual auctions. As Hake's has an exclusive worldwide clientele, we pay a high percentage of our anticipated retail to ensure a constant supply of quality collectibles for our customers. Ted Hake

Pin-Back Buttons: Political and Non-Politcal.

Our personal favorite for over 30 years. We buy buttons that relate to every category. Defects like stain, scratches and splits greatly reduce value. Here are specific offers assuming no damage whatsoever. Send photocopies.

Political

Pre-1896 lapel badges showing candidates on tin or cardboard photos	usually $100+
McKinley & Hobart on bicycle	3,000
McKinley showing factory & dinner pail	1,500
McKinley or Bryan on hobby horse	2,500
McKinley or Bryan "Eclipse" buttons	500+
Teddy Roosevelt shown with Fairbanks	usually 50+
Teddy Roosevelt shown with Johnson	1,000
James Cox 1920 picture buttons	any 100+
Cox and Franklin Roosevelt BOTH PICTURED	10,000
Truman picture on 8-ball design	4,000
Most pre-1932 picture buttons	at least 15
Votes for women & other political causes	10

Non-Political

Product advertising with pictures, pre 1920	usually $10
Farm equipment with pictures	usually 20
Mickey Mouse or Donald Duck 1930s	usually 75
Elvis Presley 1950s fan club	100
Cowboys – Tom Mix, Hoppy, Roy, Gene	usually 10
Santa Claus 1930s or earlier	usually 35
Lindbergh & early aviation	usually 15
Wonder Woman 1940s	500
Flash or U.S. Jones 1940s	ea. 500
Yellow Kid numbered series	ea. 20
Kellogg's Pep comic characters	ea. 5
Thousands of others - send photocopies	

WANTED ITEMS

Advertising: Ad figures representing Speedy Alka-Seltzer $150, Mr. Peanut wood jointed $100, Reddy Kilowatt $75+, Charlie The Tuna $15, hundreds of others. Also paper or objects from early years of famous American Companies.

Artist: From $10 for simple items to $1,000+ for original art by artists such as Disney, Vernon Grant, George Herriman, Winsor McCay, Maxfield Parrish, Richard Outcault and other comic character artists.

Autographs: Letters or signed photos of famous people like Marilyn Monroe $2,000, John Kennedy $1,000, Walt Disney $1,000 and hundreds of others.

Aviation: About anything from 1940s or earlier for real or toy airplanes or airships. World War II I.D. models $25+, Lindbergh toys or games $50+, Zeppelin souvenirs$ 25+

Baseball: Any World Series or All-Star items like programs or press pins, up to $1,000+ for early items, Hartland 1960s plastic figures $75+, bobbing head 1960s figures $25+. Nearly anything 1960s or earlier has some value.

Beatles: Any character merchandise from the 1960s such as toy guitar $150, record cases $75, lunch box 100+, also Yellow Submarine. Gum cards not wanted.

Bicycles: Lapel studs or buttons from 1900 era, each $5, League of American Wheelmen items $20+, medals for 1900 era meetings or races $25+, high wheel items, most $50+.

Big Little Books: All titles, for excellent condition $10.

Black Americana: Mechanical toys, most $100+, salt and pepper sets, most $20+, Martin Luther King signed photo $400.

Boy Scouts: Large calendars pre-1950 $25, most pinback buttons pre-1950 $10, many other items.

Boxing: Joe Louis clock or lamp $100, pre-1930s cards, each $3, famous fight program $20+.

Captain Action: Boxed figures or accessories $100+, loose figures $75, complete outfits $50+.

Cars: 1960s or earlier promotional toy models, most $50, 1930s or earlier wind-ups most $100+.

Cels: Most Disney 1950-60 $100+. Disney 1940s most $500+, also many non-Disney $100+.

Comic Characters: Almost anything depicting comic or cartoon characters from the 1970s or earlier is of interest. Prices range from $3 for Flintstone jelly glasses to $2,000 for Mickey Mouse 1930s radio.

Cowboys: All items wanted for movie and TV cowboys. Most popular are Tom Mix, Hopalong Cassidy, Roy Rogers. Prices range from $400 for Tom Mix movie posters to $75 for Bonanza lunch boxes.

Cracker Jack: Any pre-1950 paper or metal item, each $10. Not wanted–plastic items or presidential coins. Items must have company name or "C.J. Co."

Dixie Lids: Any clean condition lid, at least $3. Any 8 x 10" premium picture $5+.

Dolls: Any related to specific character or real person: Elvis 1950s $1,000, Mickey or Minnie Mouse 1930s $200+, Roy Rogers or Hopalong Cassidy $250, many others $100+.

Elvis: All items from 1956-60s era. Gum cards $3 each, toy guitar $250, wallet $100, photo ring $100, much more.

Expositions: Most pre 1970 exposition material is collected. Many items are in $5-10 range. Exception 1939 radio, $400, 1933 lamp $100, many others $25+.

Fire: Most pinback buttons or ribbon badges, pre 1930, $5-10.

GI Joe: Only want 1960-1970s large size figures and accessories. Boxed American soldiers $100+, Foreign soldiers $200+, most unboxed figures $50-100, boxed or packaged accessories, many $100+. Loose pieces also purchased.

Gum Cards: All non-baseball cards from 1960s and earlier. Many sets $100+, many individual cards $2 each.

Lunch Boxes: Metal boxes wanted from 1960s and earlier. Mickey Mouse 1930s $500, Underdog $500, Jetsons $400, Paladin $200, many others $100+.

Mirrors: Celluloid covered advertising pocket mirrors usually 2 1/2" or smaller. Colorful pictures add value. Most $25, rarities $100+.

Movies: Posters, lobby cards, games, figural objects related to pre-1950 famous stars and movies. Wizard of Oz or Gone With The Wind 1939 buttons, each $100, posters for original release of classic films, many $500+.

Pin-Ups: Calendars by Varga $50, card decks, many $25+, Playboy first issue $500, paper items by Elvgren or Moran, many $10+.

Presidential Campaigns: Snuff boxes, $500+, ribbons with portraits, most $75+, cardboard or tintype photo badges, most $100+, pin-back buttons with pictures 1896-1932, $15 each. All types of pre-1964 material wanted.

Pulp Magazines: $10-15 for titles like Weird Tales, Doc Savage, G-8, The Spider, The Shadow, Spicy Detective, many others.

Radio & Cereal Premiums: Wanted all giveaways like rings, decoders, maps, club manuals for shows like Tom Mix, Orphan Annie, Dick Tracy, The Shadow, Green Hornet, Tarzan, Space Patrol, Buck Rogers, Howdy Doody and many more. Buck Rogers knife $500, Lone Ranger 6-Gun ring $50, Orphan Annie decoder $20, Captain Marvel statuette $3,000, Superman 1940s metal ring $3,000, hundreds more worth $25-500.

Robots: Most from 1960s or earlier such as Lost In Space $200, Mr. Atomic $5,000, many $200+.

Television: Most items related to shows from 1948 - early 1970s. First TV Guide $300, Howdy Doody wood doll $250, Hopalong Cassidy cap gun $100, most board games pre-1970, $20+, most lunch boxes pre-1970 $35, dolls, many $75+, much more.

Toys: All types from 1960s and earlier. Comic character windups 1930s, most $200+, battery toys 1960s boxed, many $100+, Marx playsets complete, many $200+, Aurora monster or character model kits 1960s unbuilt, many $100+, much more.

World War II: Homefront or anti-axis items, Douglas MacArthur, Remember Pearl Harbor, V for Victory. Prefer figural objects but much paper (and Posters) also of interest. Paying $1,000 each for arcade games with anti-axis themes.

Prices are for undamaged items, paid by:

Hake's Americana & Collectibles
POB 1444 TH, York, PA 17405-1444   (717) 848-1333

All inquiries answered. Send photos or photo copies. From those we can usually make a tentative offer. Note any defects. If interested, we will provide shipping instructions. Payment is made immediately upon receipt of item, subject to revision only if the item's condition is less than anticipated when the tentative offer was made.

Lunch Boxes

I am willing to quote on all children's related items related to radio, television and movies. I buy advertising figures, tin litho, rubber, cast iron, plastic, wind-up toys, battery operated or friction. Especially items in the following categories: lunchboxes from the 1950's-1960's, robots, Barbie and GI Joe dolls with plastic formed hair, Beatles, Kiss, Jetsons, Lost in Space, Hopalong Cassidy, Gene Autry, Pez candy dispensers, Brady Bunch, Howdy Doody, vinyl advertising figures and store displays, Reddy Kilowatt, Tonka trucks, hot wheels cars with red stripe tires, slot cars, Green Hornet, Disney, monster model kits or any character related items 1970 and earlier.

Here is a sample of what I'll pay for some items in excellent to mint condition.

Metal Lunchboxes

Green hornet	$300
Lost in Space	350
Brady Bunch	100
Dr. Seuss	100
Underdog	400
E.T.	10
Strawberry Shortcake	5
Flintstones & Dino	100
Airport	500
Firehouse	200
Cablecar	200
Schoolbus	30

Hot wheels with red stripe tires in excellent to mint condition

Lola GT	$10
Classic Cord	50
Sidekick	35
Volkswagen Bus	25
S'Cool Bus	50
Splittin Image	10
Show-off	30
Prowler	30
Red Baron	15

GI Joe and Barbie Dolls in excellent to mint condition

Captain Action	$50
Japanese	150
Brunette haired Barbie with shoulder length hair	250
#1 Barbie (first one ever made)	1,200
Aquaman	75
Negro	200
Marine	50
Twiggy	40

Pez

Santa (no feet)	$20
Casper	50
Doctor	25
Indian	20-50
Bozo	45
Bullwinkle	80

Western

Roy Rodgers Guitar	$50-100
Lone Ranger cap gun	40-80
Hopalong Cassidy bike	600-1,000
Lone Ranger cap gun	40-80
Tom Mix rocking horse	75-200

Prices Paid by: Mark Blondy
Box 865
Royal Oak, MI 48068   (810) 646-8215
It's helpful to have the item in front of you when you call if I have further questions. Please inform me of any rust, scratches, dents and state of operation or send photo.

Pez, Premiums & Advertising

PEZ ITEMS – DISPENSERS

Regular (no head) with advertising	$350
Shooting star regular	1,000
"Pez Box Trademark" regular	500
"Pez Box Patent" regular	300
Witch regular (2 witch pictures on sides)	900
Old man with large white beard (Mueslix)	750
1962 Lions Club	500
Pineapple with sun glasses	450
1982 Knoxville World's Fair	500
Make-A-Face (unopened in package)	1,200
Eye in yellow flower	500
Full body shiny gold robot	750
Easter bunny (with picture on side)	250
Pink or yellow head pony	250
Capt. Hook, Mickey Mouse, Goofy, Dumbo with "Hong Kong" on head itself	400 ea.

PEZ – OTHER ITEMS

Space trooper display box	$500
Witch regular display box	1,000
Psychedelic Pez display box	500
Arithmetic display box	500
Bullwinkle display box	350
Universal monsters display box	500
Coffee flavor candy wrapper	50

PREMIUMS – RADIO & CEREAL

Superman wood statue (5-6" tall)	$1,200
Supermen of America action comics patch (round)	1,000
Supermen of America strength-courage-justice patch (square)	1,000
Supermen of America member ring	10,000
Superman secret compartment ring	10,000
Superman H-O Oats cereal box	1,000
Operator 5 ring (skull with "5")	1,500
Little Orphan Annie altascope ring	3,000
Little Orphan Annie secret guard magnifying ring	1,000
Flash comics pin	350
Wonder Woman comics pin	350
Capt. Marvel wood statue	2,000
1940s Superman bread advertising signs	200-1,000
Capt. Marvel family statues (R.W. Kerr Co.), boxed	800 ea.
Capt. Marvel Jr., Mary Marvel wood statues	1,000 ea.
Buck Rogers cut-out adventure book (unused)	700
Buck Rogers repeller ray ring (ship with stone)	1,000

PREMIUMS CON'T

Green Hornet strikes again button	250
Kix cereal box showing atomic bomb ring on front	500
Tarzan radio club drink more milk bracelet	450

ADVERTISING FIGURES

Stokely Van Camps	$200
Ready Kilowatt plastic bank	200
McGregor Happy Foot	200
Kid Reliance ashtray	250
Quisp (cereal) ceramic bank	300
(Just call me) Squirt	200
(Now's the time for) Jello	250
Chiquita Banana	250
Sonny's Dilly Burgers ashtray	325

CARTOON MOVIE POSTERS

Winsor McCay's Gertie the Dinosaur	$12,500
Alice in the Jungle (Disney)	5,000
Mickey Mouse "Columbia Pictures presents…", drawn by UB Iwerks"	10,000 up
Mickey Mouse (1930s United Artists)	5,000-10,000 ea.
Mickey Mouse theatre standee (1930s)	10,000
Donald Duck autograph hound	5,000
Disney's Mother Goose Goes to Hollywood	2,500
MGM presents Flip the Frog	2,500
Superman theatre standee, early 1940s	10,000

Always interested in rare and quality items in these categories.
Special interest in original packaging and store signs and displays related.
Condition is critical. Some of the listed items in bad shape
may not be of any interest at all.

Prices Paid by: David Welch
2308 Clay St., P.O. Box 714
Murphysboro, IL 62966

(618) 687-2282
FAX (618) 684-2243

Comic Book Art

There have been 17,000+ comic books published since the 1930's. My specialty is in the pre-1975 artwork made to produce these .

Artists drew in two sizes: (1) 13"x18" up until mid-1967, and (2) 10"x15" from then on. The artists I seek are listed with their most popular characters. They drew others, but prices paid for lesser characters are 30%-60% of prices quoted below. Price ranges reflect drawing quality and graphic interest which varies from picture to picture.

Please send Xeroxes or photos of all items. It will help me determine who drew the art and if there are any problems to its condition. Both Superman and Batman have had hundreds of artists. I am interested in many of them beyond those listed.

	Interior	Cover
Jack Kirby		
Fantastic Four, X-men, Thor, Captain America, Challengers of the Unknown	$50-1,000	$750-3,000
Steve Ditko		
Spiderman, Dr. Strange, Horror Stories, Blue Beetle	100-1,500	1,000-4000
Curt Swan		
Superman	50-200	600-1,500
Bob Kane		
Batman	2,000-5,000	5,000-10,000
Note: He had many assistants, and after 1947 very little art is actually Bob Kane. These prices are 10-20% of Bob Kane's.		
Lou Fine		
Uncle Sam, The Ray, Dollman, Black Condor	200-500	1,000-3,000
Neal Adams		
X-Men, Deadman, Batman, Green Lantern	50-250	500-1,500
Carmine Infantino		
Batman The Flash, Adam Strange	50-250	1,000-2,500
Carl Barks		
Uncle Scrooge, Donald Duck,	1,000-2,000	2,000-4,000
Note: Most of his covers are smaller than comic book interior pages.		
Robert Crumb		
Mr. Natural, Fritz the Cat	250-500	1,000-2,500
Gil Kane		
Atom, Green Lantern	20-200	200-1,500
Joe Kubert		
Sgt. Rock, Viking Prince	50-200	300-1,500
John Romita		
Spiderman	20-200	200-1,500
Joe Shuster		
Superman	200-1,000	5,000-10,000

Price paid: $1,500

Comic Strip Art

Unlike the comic book art, comic strips are usually signed and dated, and more easy to identify. The size drawn varies widely. Sunday pages range from a size of 10"x15" to 24"x36". The daily strips can be 3"x10" up to 8"x30". Like comic books, these are black and white pen and ink drawings. Occasionally originals were colored, but these are uncommon. Each artist has a period their work that is more desirable. Normally, it is their early work. These have the higher value.

	Daily	Sunday		Daily	Sunday
V.T. Hamlin			**Harold Gray**		
Alley Oop	$20-300	$100-1,500	Little Orphan		
Billy De Beck			Annie	$100-600	$300-2,000
Barney Google	75-150	200-800	**Mickey Mouse**		
Dick Calkins			Pre-1940 only	500-2,000	1,000-5,000
Buck Rogers	250-2,000	1,000-2,500	**Charles Schulz**		
Murphy Anderson			Peanuts	200-600	800-1,500
Buck Rogers	100-250	500-750	**McCoy or Moore**		
Chester Gould			The Phantom,		
Dick Tracy	100-500	600-2,500	Pre-1950	100-500	400-1,000
Donald Duck			**Walt Kelly**		
Pre-1950 only	200-600	500-1,500	Pogo	200-400	500-1,000
Alex Raymond			**Hal Foster**		
Flash Gordon	-	2,000-10,000	Prince Valiant		1,000-5,000
Dan Barry			Tarzan	500-1000	2,000-5,000
Flash Gordon,			**E.C. Segar**		
1952-4 only	100-250		Popeye	200-600	1,000-2,500
George Herriman			**Burne Hogarth**		
Krazy Kat	500-1,000	2,000-5,000	Tarzan	-	2,000-5,000
Windsor McCay			**Milton Caniff**		
Little Nemo in			Terry & the Pirates	100-300	500-1,500
Slumberland	-	2,500-7,500			

Prices Paid by: Tom Horvitz
21520 Burbank, #315
Woodland Hills, CA 91367

FAX (818) 347-2357
(818) 716-8664

Radios

The development of the radio industry was rapid during the years 1921 to 1940. Radios went through many physical changes and circuits designs in this short period. It is the period of time that most collectors of radios concentrate on. In the early 1920's radios were mainly of the battery operated type, usually contained in a wooden case with a lift-top lid. After 1928 almost all radios were plugged into an AC wall outlet. Cabinet styles can usually be used to date most radios.

RADIOS WANTED:

1921 to 1927 battery operated radios – models with 1 to 3 tubes	$30-300
1921 to 1927 battery operated radios – models with 4 to 8 tubes	40-175
1920's crystal radios (use no tubes), must be factory made!	25-200
1928 to 1930 AC operated table models, wood cabinets only	25-75
1928 to 1930 AC operated table models, metal cabinets	10-35
1930 to 1934 cathedral shaped radios (rounded tops)	50-200
1930 to 1938 tombstone shaped radios (tall w/flat top)	35-100
1930's floor models (not usually bought unless exceptional)	25-150
1930's table or mantle sets (small radios less than 12" wide)	10-50

Radios of bakelite or plastic are not wanted unless of unusual design.

RADIO SPEAKERS:

Horn type used with 1920's radios	$25-95
1920's cone speakers (round, open framed paper front type)	20-75
1930's speakers enclosed in wood or metal cabinets	10-25

RADIO LITERATURE:

Riders Service manuals, Volumes 1-23	$7-20
1920/30's radio catalogs such as Barawik, Allied, Lafayette	5-20
1920' radio magazines: Radio News, Popular Radio, Radio Broadcast	3-10
1930's radio magazines: Radio Craft, Short-Wave Craft, others	2-5

Note: during the 1920/30's there were over 40 titles of magazines

RADIO TUBES & PARTS:

Buy most early 4-prong radio tubes, either new or used, and most other tubes up to 1940 if new. Because there are thousands of different types made it is impossible to give an accurate range of prices. Also buy all types of radio parts for the servicing and repair of radios such as transformers, dials, knobs, new-old-stock parts.

As items wanted are of a very technical nature it is very helpful it complete description of items is given. Sketches or photos of radios are helpful. Will pay for all photos or other costs you incur to send complete information.

Also buy early tipped light bulbs, telegraph items, old phones, radio advertising signs and ephemera.

Prices Paid by: Gary Schneider
14310 Ordner Drive
Cleveland, Ohio 44136   (After 9 PM) (216) 582-3094

Movie Posters

I will pay the following prices for American 1-Sheets (27" x 41") in excellent condition:

American Graffiti - 40x60 or larger	Ea. $60
Angels With Dirty Faces	3,000
Animal House - 40x60 or larger	Ea. 60
Animal Crackers	4,000
Baby Takes a Bow	3,000
Black Cat (1934) - 1-Sheet	25,000
Black Pirate (Fairbanks)	5,000
Blue Angel - 1-Sheet or Larger	Ea. 10,000
Bordertown	500
Breakfast at Tiffany's - 1-Sheet	500
Bride of Frankenstein - 1-Sheet	60,000
Bringing Up Baby	2,500
Broken Arrow - 1-Sheet	75
Cabaret - 3-Sheet or larger	Ea. 60
Captain Blood	3,000
Casablanca	3,000
Citizen Kane	9,000
Cleopatra (1934) Full-length Colbert 3-Sheet	6,000
Creature from Black Lagoon1 Sheet or larger	Ea. 2,000
Crime School	2,000
Dangerous	4,000
Day the Earth Stood Still 1-Sheet or larger	Ea. 2,500
Dinner at 8 - 22x28 or 1-Sheet	Ea. 5,000
Dr. Jekyll & Mr. Hyde (Barrymore - 1920)	24,000
Dr. Jekyll & Mr. Hyde (1932) 1-Sheet or larger	Ea. 18,000
Dracula insert	20,000
Dracula	65,000
Enter the Dragon - 40x60 or larger	Ea. 60
Flying Down to Rio - 1-Sheet	10,000
Footlight Parade	4,000
Frankenstein (style A or B)	80,000
Frankenstein - 1-Sheet	72,000
General, The	12,000
Girl From 10th Avenue	6,000

Gold Rush	15,000
Gold Diggers of 1935	3,000
Gone With The Wind	5,000
Gone with the Wind - 40x60 or 3-Sheet	Ea. 6500
Graduate - 1-Sheet or larger	Ea. 50
Hallelujah!	4,500
Hound of the Baskervilles (1939) 1-Sheet or 3-Sheet	Ea. 6,000
Hunchback of Notre Dame (Chaney)	16,000
Invisible Ray - 1-Sheet	16,000
Invisible Man - 1-Sheet or 3-Sheet	Ea. 25,000
It's a Wonderful Life-1-Sheet or larger	Ea. 3,000
Jesse James - 1-Sheet or larger	Ea. 2,000
Jezebel - 1-Sheet or 3-Sheet	Ea. 6000
King Kong (1933) - 1-Sheet or larger	Ea. 42,000
King Kong Press Book	1,800
Little Caesar	13,000
London After Midnight	20,000
London After Midnight title card	4,000
Lost World	20,000
Maltese Falcon	3,000
Man From - Planet X	2,000
Mark of Zorro (1940) 1-Sheet or larger	Ea. 3,000
Mata Hari	4,500
Metropolis (American release)	60,000
Mummy insert	20,000
Mummy, The (style C or D)	70,000
Mummy, The 1/2 Sheet	20,000
Old Dark House	30,000
Out of the Past (1947) 1-Sheet or larger	Ea. 1,000
Petrified Forest - 1-Sheet or larger	Ea. 5,000
Public Enemy - 1-Sheet	21,000
Puttin' On The Ritz	3,000
Raven (1935) - 1-Sheet	25,000
Razor's Edge (1946) Norman Rockwell 1-Sheet or 3-Sheet	Ea. 1500
Rebecca	1,800
Rocky Horror Picture Show	50
Roman Holiday - 1-Sheet	100
Sabrina - 1-Sheet	100
Scarlet Empress (artwork) 22x28 or Larger	Ea. 5,000
Shane - 1-Sheet (near mint)	500
Son of Frankenstein	5,500
Son of Kong	13,000
Steamboat Willie	60,000
Superman (1941 Fleischer)	5,000
Superman & the Mole Men	1,000
Tale of Two Cities (1935) - 1-Sheet	3,000
The 39 Steps	3,000
Thin Man - 22x28 or larger	2,500
This Gun For Hire	2,800
War of the Worlds - 1/2 Sheet w/saucers	2,000
War of the Worlds - British Quad	2,000
Werewolf of London	17,000
Winchester '73 - Insert/22x28/1-Sheet	Ea. 100
Wizard of Oz	4,000
Wolfman	5,500

Prices Paid by: Dwight Cleveland
P.O. Box 10922
Chicago, IL 60610

Magic Posters & Memorabilia

I have been actively collecting vintage magic posters and related magicians' memorabilia and ephemera for the past 20 years. It is difficult to put a price on all posters of a particular performer or all posters in a particular category because there may be a great difference in value between a rare poster and a more common one. Therefore, the prices set out below may be close to what I am willing to pay. So contact me and I will make you an offer after I know the specifics about your poster.

Especially with paper items, condition is all important. If something is not properly mounted or is badly torn or folded, stained, etc., it may lower the value of the item. A color photo is always helpful in evaluating an item.

EXAMPLES OF SPECIFIC MAGICIANS WHOSE POSTERS I BUY.
ALL ITEMS ARE FULL COLOR STONE LITHOGRAPHS.

Price Paid $700+ each

Albini	$350+
Andress	300+
Bancroft	500+
Blackstone Sr.	300+
Brindamour	350+
Brush	300+
Carter (Goes litho)	400+
Chung Ling Soo	500+
Dante	400+
T. Nelson Downs	500+
Germain (Germaine)	500+
Goldin	375+
Hardeen	400+
Herrmann	750+
Houdini	1000+
Kellar	650+
Servais Leroy	400+
Maro	350+
Nicola	375+
Powell	500+
Raymond	500+
Rameses	500+
Rouclere	400+
Thurston (Otis)	350+
Thurston (Strobridge)	600+
Valadon	500+
Von Arx	300+
Wood	500+

This is not intended to be a complete list. If you have a poster of a magician not named on this list, call or write anyway... I also collect stock posters issued by litho companies. These may not always have the name of a specific performer but are still of some interest to me.

I am not interested in posters depicting Carter (Otis litho), George, Heaney, Irving, Fak Hong or Kar-Mi unless your price is very low. I am not interested in reproductions of posters or contemporary magic posters such as David Copperfield.

OTHER MAGIC EPHEMERA & MEMORABILIA

Childrens' magic sets, including Mysto, Aladdin, Spear. Expecially interested in English, French & German sets. 25-250, depending on rarity, condition, etc. Sets that are mostly plastic from the 1950's or later are usually of little interest.

Houdini collectibles – photos, letters and postcards, scrapbooks, paper advertising, clippings, handcuffs, books and pamphlets, signed or unsigned items, $35-500 or more, depending on the item, rarity and condition. Not interested in *Big Little Books.*

Programmes, Broadsides and other magic magicians' advertising- 50¢ to $500 paid, depending on the item, its condition and rarity.

Give-aways from magicians-postcards, signed photos, pinbacks, tokens, throw-out cards, pamphlets, door-hangers, sheet music, handbills etc. $3-300, depending on item, rarity and condition.

Product advertising and character items with a magic theme - For example, Mickey Mouse Magician tin toy, magician bank.

Prints & Engravings with magic themes - $5-500, depending on rarity and condition.

Magic apparatus in good condition manufactured before 1950- Prices depend on condition and scarcity. It is helpful if instructions are included.
Home-made apparatus is usually of little value. Also, I am not looking for jokes or puzzles.

Hard-cover books $1-1,000 paid, depending on the book.

Soft cover magic books, pre-1900- $10-1,000, depending on the book, its condition and scarcity.

Magic magazines- Only interested in complete runs of early (pre-1920) magazines. $50-500 for the run, depending on the magazine. Not interested in *Genii, Linking Ring, MUM* or *Tops*.

Magic catalogs- Only pre-1925 catalogs in good shape $25-250, depending on the catalog, its condition & rarity.

Price paid: $1,000+ each

Price paid: $600+ each

Prices Paid by:	Ken Trombly	(202) 887-5000
	1825 K Street, NW, Suite 901	FAX (202) 457-0343
	Washington, D.C. 20006	
	Toll free (to sell me posters) 1-800-673-8158	

Please don't send anything on approval –call or write first .

Vintage 78 rpm Phonograph Records

Most everyone has a stack of old 78's somewhere - in the closet, basement, barn or attic. However, only a very small percentage have significant value, and condition is as important in this field as in any other. Rare records are often encountered, however. So records are definitely worth checking out before they are given away. The following information will give you a general idea of what to look for.

(All prices quoted are for records in excellent condition.)

JAZZ, BLUES, CAJUN AND COUNTRY RECORDS FROM 1925-1935

There are literally thousands of artists and labels in this category that are of significant value. The following label series each contain records that could be valued at $20, $50, even $100 or more!

Brunswick (lightning bolt label) 100-500 and 7000 series
Bluebird (buff-colored label) 2000 and 5000 series
Champion 15-16,000 series
Columbia 14-15,000 series
Gennett 5-7,000 series
Okeh 8,000; 40-41,000 and 45,000 series
Paramount 3,000 and 12-13,000 series
Perfect 0100-0200 series
Victor 23,000; V-38,000; and V-40,000 series
Vocalion 1-5000 and 14-15,000 series

Emil Cassi. Berliner $75

Please note that not every record that falls within these number ranges has collector value, but a great many do. Further, there are many more jazz, blues, Cajun and country records that are very valuable which are not found in this list!

EARLY CLASSICAL AND OPERATIC RECORDS MADE PRIOR TO 1910

Red label Victor "Monarch" or "Deluxe" records	$20-100
One-sided Columbia "Grand Opera" disc records	150-500
Fonotipia or Odeon records	10-500
Gramophone & Typewriter label records	15-1,000
Operatic Zonophone records	20-1,500

Please note that later classical records and album sets are generally of lesser value and are therefore usually of little interest.

PICTURE RECORDS

Vogues	$20-1,000
RCA Victors	150-2,000
7" Children's Picture Records	5-25
Mercurys	150
Talk-O-Photos	200
Other Picture Discs	5-500

RCA Victor Picture Disc $400

Generally speaking, we want any 78 rpm picture record you have, regardless of scarcity, value or condition.

ODD AND UNUSUAL LABELS

Herwin	Flexo
Herschel	Sunrise
Black Patti	Superior
Electra	Polk
Electradisk	Merritt
QRS	Buddy
Vitaphone	Nation's Forum
Black Swan	Wonder
Kalamazoo	Blu-Disc
KKK	Berliner
Autograph	Sunshine
Gem	Harmograph
Timely Tunes	Rialto
Hollywood	Sun
Vulcan	Phonolamp
Nordskog	Chautauqua

This is only a partial list! I will pay $10-300 for examples of these labels in excellent condition.

EARLY ROCK AND ROLL FROM THE 1950'S

Look for labels like Sun, Imperial, Checker, Jubilee, Specialty, etc., and for artists like Buddy Holly, Elvis Presley, Chuck Berry and Little Richard. Prices paid will range from $3-250, but records must be in excellent condition with very little or no wear!

CYLINDER RECORDS

Brown wax cylinders	$5-100
Pink, purple, white or orange celluloid cylinders	50-200
Any cylinders measuring 6" in length or 5" in diameter	50-100
Any blue cylinders numbered between 5000 and 5750	5-50
Any cylinders with operatic or historical content	5-100

Do not attempt to clean your cylinders. Avoid touching the surface of the cylinder with your fingers, as this could cause major problems as well. DO NOT attempt to play your cylinders, as they can easily be ruined by improper equipment!

Important!
We do not buy the following types of music: big band, Hawaiian, sacred, popular and traditional songs, popular instrumental selections or album sets. We also do not buy 45 or 33 long play records!

**We are also interested in purchasing wind-up phonographs
and antique music boxes!**

Prices Paid by: Nauck's Vintage Records
6323 Inway Drive   (713) 370-7899
Spring, TX 77389   FAX (713) 251-7023

If you would like a copy of our illustrated want list with additional categories included, please send $2.00 plus a legal-sized SASE. This brochure will also include instructions for listing, packing and shipping your records. If the size and value of your collection warrants it, we will be happy to travel to your location for an on-site evaluation!

Phonograph Records

Most records on the following labels are of little to no interest or value to collectors. Of course, there are exceptions - collectible records - on each label listed.

Budget labels, such as CLUB 45, 18 TOP HITS, GILMAR, TOPS, TOP 30 TUNES, and VALUE, are often multi-track, featuring "covers" of popular, hit tunes by artists other than those who recorded the hit version.

Capitol	Mercury
Columbia (red label)	MGM
Coral	Musicraft
Decca (black label)	Okeh (purple label)
London	RCA Victor

RECORDS OF OTHER LABELS:

If your records are made after 1940 or are on other labels, describe generally what you have (labels; artist; speed: 78, 45, LP; etc.). If you've already compiled a list, send it (include self-addressed, stamped envelope for its return); if you haven't yet made a list, read my wants list or other info I'll send you in exchange for a SASE.

"SHELLAC SHACK'S WANT LIST OF 78 RPM RECORDS":

For the information and convenience of sellers, I offer my copyrighted, 72-page booklet, which contains buying prices for thousands of 78 RPM records on commonly found labels (such as Bluebird, Brunswick, Columbia, Decca, Victor, etc.), listed by record number with the specific price I pay for each disc. This is a detailed, "live" buying offer, backed by cash - not a vague reference. Included are pictures of many labels, packing and shipping information. This booklet is sent for $2.00 which is refunded when records are sold to me. It is not necessary, however, to buy the booklet or anything else from me in order to offer/sell me records.

> **"American Premium Record Guide"** by L.R. Docks, published by Books Americana, will provide those interested with a more comprehensive view of popular record collecting. It lists 78s, 45s, and LPs, 1900-1965, including jazz, blues, dance bands, hillbilly, rock 'n' roll, rhythm & blues, rockabilly, celebrity recordings, etc. Included are 1400 label photographs, a bibiliography and list of publications. Check your bookstore, or write to me for more information.

OLD PHONOGRAPH RECORDS 78 RPM AND OTHERS
Pre-1940 Scarce, Interesting and Unusual Labels and Series

Following are some scarce labels, and special series, all of which are wanted, regardless of musical content or lack thereof. All are pre-1940, and should not be confused with more modern labels having the same or similar names. For illustrations of most of these, and many other labels, see my booklet, "Shellac Shack's Want List of 78 RPM Records," described elsewhere, and/or my book, "American Premium Record Guide." Prices are minimums, for the most common issues on each label; "better" issues will be bought at higher prices (sometimes multiples of quoted prices). Labels of records should be clean and free of significant damage, such as writing, stickers, and needle scratching (records should be in nice, playable condition); this is especially important with respect to many of the following records.

Label	Price	Label	Price
Ajax (Canada)	$4	Moxie	$10
Aurora (Canada)	5	Mozart (St. Louis)	3
Autograph (Marsh Lab., Chicago)	4	*National (Iowa City)	2
Berliner (7",single-sided, embossed "label")	8	New Flexo (small, flexible disc)	5
Black Patti (Chicago Record Co.)	50	*Nordskog	6
*Blu Disc (#T001 through T-1009)	25	Odeon (American "ONY" Series"	4
*Buddy (Six cities/companies		Paramount (12000 and 13000 series)	4
mentioned on label)	20	Parlophone (American "PNY" Series)	4
Carnival (John Wanamaker, NY)	10	Par-o-ket (7-inch, embossed "label")	4
Chappelle & Stinette	10	Pennington (Bamberger & Co., New Jersey)	4
Chautauqua (Washington, D.C.)	10	Personal Record (by Columbia; "-P" series)	2
Clover (Nutmeg Record Co.)	3	Q.R.S. (Cova Recording Co., New York)	5
Connorized	2	R.C.A. Victor "Program Transcription"	4
Dandy	4	R.C.A. Victor Picture Discs	10
Davega	2	Rialto (Rialto Music House, Chicago)	10
Davis & Schwegler	5	Stark	5
Domestic (Philadelphia)	5	*Sunrise	3
Edison ("Needle Cut Electric")	6	*Sunrise (R.C.A. Victor product)	20
Edison (Long-playing 24-minute)	10	*Sunset ("made in California U.S.A.")	3
Edison (Long-playing 40-minute, 12 inch)	15	*Sunshine (St. Petersburg, FL)	5
Edison (Sample record, 12-inch)	20	*Sunshine (Los Angeles, CA)	10
Electradisk	2	*Superior	4
Everybodys	3	Timely Tunes (R.C.A. Victor product)	5
Flexo (small, flexible disc,		Tremont (American Record Mfg.)	2
by Pacific Coast Record Corp., San Francisco)	6	Up-To-Date	2
*Golden (Los Angeles)	5	Victor 23000 - 23041, inclusive	3
Gramophone (See "Berliner," above)		Victor 23250 - 23432, inclusive	5
Herschel Gold Seal	5	Victor 23500 - 23859, inclusive	2
Herwin (St. Louis)	5	Victor V-38000 - V-38146, inclusive	3
*Hollywood Record (California)	5	Victor V-38500 - V-38631, inclusive	5
Homestead (Chicago Mail Order)	5	Yerkes	4
Improved (7-inch, single-sided,			
by Eldridge R. Johnson)	8	*particularly susceptible to confusion with more	
Marathon (7-inch, by Nutmeg Record Corp.)	6	modern, similarly named labels.	
*Meritt (Kansas City)	25		

Prices Paid by: L.R. "Les" Docks
P.O. Box 691035
San Antonio, Texas 78269

Musical Instruments

Paying cash for guitars by Gibson, Gretsch, Fender, Martin, Rickenbacker, Epiphone, Stromberg, D'Angelico, D'Aquisto, Guild, Vox, National, Dobro, Maurer, Prairie State, etc. Interested in all used, vintage American instruments - banjos, amps, mandolins, ukuleles, etc. Prices are guidelines for clean, original instruments. Modifications lower value as much as 50%.

FENDER GUITARS

Fender guitars were made in Fullerton, California as were amplifiers and other musical instruments. All US-made Fender instruments are of interest and have some value. Among them, these are the most significant. Dates of manufacture are determined by serial numbers and markings.

Fender Stratocaster Guitars

1950's maple fingerboard, sunburst finish	$3,000-6,000
1960's rosewood fingerboard, sunburst finish	2,500 up
1960's rosewood fingerboard, solid color	3,500 up
1970's large headstock, three bolt neck	350-1,200
More if hardware is gold plated.	

Fender Telecaster or Esquire Guitars

1950's Broadcaster, see thru butterscotch	$5,000-10k
1950's maple fingerboard, lemon finish, orig.	2,500-5,000
1960's rosewood fingerboard, lemon finish	1,500-2,500
1960's rosewood fingerboard, solid color	2,500-4,000
1960's sunburst with white binding on body	2,000-3,000
1960's paisley floral finish on body	1,800-2,500
More if hardware is gold plated.	

Fender Jaguar & Jazzmaster Guitars

1960's sunburst finish, all original	$600-up
1960's solid colors (blue, red, gold, white, etc.)	800-up
More if hardware is gold plated.	

Fender Lap Steel Guitars

(Electric Hawaiian Guitars)

1950's six or eight strings, any finish	$100-450

Fender Basses

1960's Jazz Bass, sunburst finish	$600-1,800
1950's Precision Bass, sunburst finish	900-1,500
1960's Precision Bass, sunburst finish	500-1,000

GRETSCH GUITARS

Most Gretsch guitars are worth $100-500. Some of the finer models listed below, if original, are worth considerably more. Prices are for unmodified examples with original cases. Value is higher if original advertising is included (catalog, price tag, invoice, photos, strap, etc.), and lower if modified.

50's White Penguin, white solid body	$10,000 up
50's White Falcon, single cutaway	3,500-8,000
60's White Falcon, double cutaway	1,500-3,000
50's Country Gentleman, single cutaway	2,000-2,500
50's Chet Atkins 6120, orange, single cutaway	2,000-35,000
50's Roundup, orange, "B" brand, solid body	1,400-2,500
50's-60's Duo Jet solid body, red, sparkle	1,000-2,500
Synchromatic models, non-electric	500-2,500
Gretsch amplifiers, with western motif	400-800
Gretsch advertising, clocks, signs, catalogs	100-500

GIBSON Les Paul Model Guitars

Most all Gibson guitars are valued above $200. Some models are very valuable if all original and ummodified. Additionally, old instruments in poor condition have value for parts with some 1950's parts alone worth over $500! Naturally, an appraisal is worthwhile.

50's-60's sunburst Les Paul standard	$15,000 up
50's gold top, white pickups (P-90's)	3,000-10,000
50's gold top, metal pickups (Humbuckers)	10,000 up
60's gold top, white pickups (P-90's)	800-1,800
50's Les Paul Junior, sunburst or red finish	950-1,500
50's Les Paul TV model, yellow finish	1,200-2,000
70's Les Paul Deluxe, custom, standard	500 up
80's Les Paul Custom, standard	500 up

GIBSON GUITARS

20's L-5 archtop, Loar signature, dot inlays	$3,000-up
30's-50's L-5 archtop guitar, no pickups	2,000-up
30's EB-150 "Charlie Christian" model, pickup	2,000-up
30's-40's Super 400 guitar, no pickups	5,000-up
60's Super 400 CES, L-5CES, with pickups	4,000-up
59 ES-335TDN, natural finish, dot inlay	$3,500-8,000
59 ES-34STDN, natural finish	3,000-6,000
58-62 ES-335, dot inlay, stop TPC, sunburst	2,000-5,000
62-69 ES-335, orange label	950-2,000
50's Flying V guitar, solid body, "V" shaped	20,000 up
50's Explorer guitar, solid body, "Z" shaped	20,000 up
30's J-200 guitar, flat top, rosewood body	10,000 up
30's jumbo guitar, flat top, rosewood body	5,000 up

MARTIN GUITARS

All Martin guitars are valuable. Prices range from $300 for the all mahogany Q-15 model to $20,000 for the pre-WWII D-45 model with abalone borders. Martin ukes are worth at least $150-900, for most models. Martin mandolins are worth far less unless ornamented. Prices below are for the most desirable models which I'm always interested in buying.

30's-40's s000-45, pearl trim, rosewood each	$5,000-10,000
60's D-45, pearl trim, rosewood back	8,000 up
30's D-28, rosewood back and sides	6,000-15,000
40's D-28, rosewood back and sides	4,000-10,000
50's D-28, rosewood back and sides	2,000-3,500
30's OM-28, rosewood back and sides	5,000-9,500
30's OM-45, pearl trim, rosewood	9,000-15,000
39-42 D-45, pearl trim, rosewood	20,000 up
20's-30's Hawaiian models	500-2,500

KOAWOOD MODELS, TENORS, ARCHTOPS, FLAT TOPS, ALL MODELS BOUGHT.

OTHER MAKERS

30's-50's D'Angelico guitars, any original	$7,500-20K
30's-50's Stromberg guitars, any original	7,500-25K
60's Rickenbacker guitars, 6 or 12 string	500-1,800
30's National metal body guitars, ukes, mandolins	500-5,000

AMPLIFIERS

50's Fender Bassman, tweed covering, 4-10" speakers	$800-1,000
50's Fender Super, tweed coveirng	550-1,000
60's Vox AC30 w /top boost, combo w/ stand	500-1,000
500's Fender tweed amps, all models	250 up++
60's Fender Vobrolux reverb, deluxe, super	300 up++
60's Marshall amplifiers, half-stacks, stacks	900-1,500
30's-60's Gibson amplifiers, all original	150 1,000

BANJOS

20's-30's Gibson Mastertone banjos	$900-6,500
20's-30's BAcon and Day Silverbell banjos	700-7,500
20's-30's Paramount banjos	450-4,500
20's-30's Vega banjos	150-4,500
1900's Fairbanks banjos, Whyte Laydie, etc.	350-9,000
1900's S.S. Stewart banjos, fancy inlays	500-5,000
20's Ludwig banjos, banjo-ukes	250-2,500

Please note: I am a serious buyer and do not intend to "trifle" with serious sellers. I 'll pay cash for good instruments, accurately and honestly described. If you have or know of an instrument for sale, call with a full description including serial number and asking price. Serious finders are encouraged to contact me. If I buy the instrument, I will pay all shipping costs plus reimburse you for your phone call to me!

Prices Paid by: Steve Senerchia
91 Tillinghast Ave.
Warwick, RI 02886

(401) 821-2865
FAX (401) 823-1612

If I am not at the phone please leave a message. I will return your call as soon as I get back. Don't forget to leave your number!

SENERCHIA

Golf

Golf Clubs, Memorabilia & Golfing Antiques

Collector of good original quality equipment. Prefer unrestored, refinished, cleaned and repaired items.

Common wood shaft clubs from 1915-1937 were manufactured in the millions. Of these, 70-85% of them have value of $5-50 in general. Most have no collector interest other than being wall hangers. Some of these makers are Wilson, Spalding, Mcgregor, Burke, H&B. Common clubs have marks such as dot punched faces, dot-dash faces, caps at grip end of shafts, heads marked with yardage, head marked match set, chrome plated heads.

Common Wood Shafts, 1915-1937

Woods	$5-50
Irons	5-20
Putters	10-75
Smooth face clubs (irons)	115-120
Spalding spring face	250-1,200
Spalding cran iron (wood insert on face)	200-1,200
Spalding Seely patent irons	300-1,000
Hagen concave face sand club	150-450
Spalding, Macgregor, Wright & Ditson, Burke, Forgan and many other splice neck woods	75-500+

Spliced Woods

by makers McEwan, Park, Simpson, The Spalding, Morris, Dunn, Scott, etc.	$220-1,200

Long Nose Play Clubs

Mid-1800 thru 1890's – Allan, Philp, Anderson, Ayres, Dunn, Forgan, Gibson, Park, Patrick, etc.	$200-2100+

Classic Clubs 1940-1970's

Drivers	$50-150
Wood sets	150-500
Iron sets	75-500

Seeking top quality playable classic.

Macgregor Woods

M85, M75, TPT, WW Penna, SS1, 693, Armour Promodel, Hogan Promodel, George Bayer models	$75-500+
Tommy Armour putters marked silver scot ironmaster with codes as 3852, IM, IMG, IMG6, IMG5, etc.	40-450

Putters

Ping Putter, Scottsdale models B66, 67, 69, 1A, 11A, 111A, etc.	$50-250
Wilson - 8802, 8813, Arnold Palmer, etc.	250-800

Irons

Ping Ballmatic, model 69, K1, K11, K111, Ping Eye, Ping Eye 2, Ping Eye II Plus sets	$200-500+

Gold Balls

Feather balls	$300-1,500+
Gutta percha balls	30-600
Rubber core balls 1895-1930	5-100
Mesh pattern balls	5-50
Post 1935 modern balls	5-30

Golf Books

Interested in 1st printings, dated.

Prior to 1940	
Books up to 1920	$10-400+
Books 1920-1930	5-50
Books 1930-1970	5-40
Manufacturers equipment catalogues 1920-1945	10-65

China & Pottery

Many companies produced plates, jugs, multi-handled mugs, bowls, vases, humidors, beakers, match stick holders, etc.

Made by Carltonware, Copeland Spode, Doulton, Gerz, Grimwades Ltd., Lenox, Minton, O'Hara Dial Co., Sleepyeye, Wedgewood, Weller, etc.

Prices paid vary greatly depending on manufacturer, type of piece, colors used, and subject	$50-5,000

General Golf

The different golf items of interest to me are just too numerous to list. Here are a few.

Contestant badges, trophies of famous players and courses, tournament programs, autographs, early photos, tintypes, postal stamps, 1st day issues, prints, printings, pocket watches, match safes, ink stands, flasks, bookends, door stops, bronze statuary, cigarette cards, post cards of early golfers and courses. Golf games, slot machines, pinball machines, early golf films, instructional albums, etc.

Any item no matter how rare is only worth what a buyer is willing to pay. Photo copies, photographs and complete description of items offered for sale are very helpful. Sometimes item must be in hand to determine the fairest and most accurate price I can pay you.

Prices Paid by: Richard Regan
293 Winter Street, #5
Hanover, MA 02339

(617)826-3537

Baseball & Sports Memorabilia

Collecting sports memorabilia has become very popular in recent years. Old autographs, programs, team yearbooks, ticket stubs to famous or championship games or matches, pins picturing athletes and advertising posters picturing athletes are highly desirable. However, remember condition is critical. Please, feel free, to contact me if you have any sports memorabilia to sell.

Autographs

Babe Ruth	$300-2,000
Lou Gehrig	500-3,000
Roy Campanella	100-350
Roger Maris	35-200
Tris Speaker	100-1,500
Walter Johnson	150-1500
Bobby Jones (golfer)	125-700
Jack Johnson (boxer)	150-650
Ty Cobb	150-1,500
Jackie Robinson	100-350
Joe Dimaggio	20-100
Thurman Munson	75-400
Christy Mathewson	500-3,000
Roberto Clemente	75-700
Joe Louis (boxer)	50-200
Vince Lombardi (football)	75-200

I am also buying autographs of any deceased, well know athlete. Please do not offer me autographs of living athletes except for Joe Dimaggio.

Team Yearbooks

1950 NY Yankees (called a Sketch Book)	$50-125
1950's NY Yankees Yearbooks (official version only)	50-100
1955 Brooklyn Dodgers Yearbooks	50-125
1950's Brooklyn Dodgers Yearbooks	40-75
1941 Brooklyn Dodgers Yearbook	50-100
1942 Brooklyn Dodgers Yearbook	100-250
1962 NY Mets Yearbook	75-150

I am also buying other team yearbooks from the 1950's and earlier.

Programs

1903 World Series Program	$10,000 +up
1927 World Series Program	200-700
1955 World Series Program	40-75
1969 World Series Program	40-75
Super Bowl I Program	75-150

I am also buying other World Series programs before 1957 and most Super Bowl programs and championship boxing.

Ticket Stubs

1903 World Series	$1,000-2,000
1927 World Series	100-250
1955 World Series	25-50

I am also buying ticket stubs to World Series games before 1979, and stubs to any boxing and football championships. I will pay much higher prices for full unused tickets to these events.

Pins and Advertising Posters

Anything picturing Mickey Mantle, Babe Ruth, Joe Dimaggio, Roger Maris, Lou Gehrig, Ty Cobb, Joe Louis and any other well known athlete is wanted by me. Contact me if you have any of those items for sale.

Walter Johnson $450 if autographed

Ticket stub 1923 World Series $150

BABE RUTH
NEW YORK

November 7th 1947

Mr Salvatore Titone
1684- 76th Street
Brooklyn, New York.

Dear Sir:

Thank you very much for the photos
of your little son Nicholas in his baseball
togs. They are very amusing and he must be a
bright little fellow.

I would like very much to meet him
sometime although for the present I am doing
a great deal pf traveling.As a matter of fact
I have just returned from Nebraska and am leaving
town on another assignment tomorrow.

In the meantime I am sending the little
fellow an autographed picture for his album.

With best wishes,

Sincerely,

Babe Ruth
Babe Ruth

110 Riverside Drive
New York City, NY

Will pay $1,200

Note: Prices of letters are determined by contents.

Prices Paid by: Richard Simon
215 East 80th Street
New York, NY 10021

(212) 988-1349
FAX (212) 288-1445

Sports

Curator of the Monterey Bay Sports Museum is buying memorabilia

We are always looking to increase our displays, and I'll pay the following prices in order to enhance the museum:

Any and all 19th century advertising/ display posters that depict sports figures, sports card sets, testimonials for products of the time	$1,000-100,000 cash
An original set/pair of 19th cen. fingerless baseball gloves	1,000-1500
19th cen. baseball bats	200 up
Pre-1940 felt pennants from football, baseball and boxing matches	50-1,000 ea.
19th century football uniform	1000
Especially interested in larger display items, such as large banners and display pieces	500 up
Tickets: full tickets and stubs	
1910 Johnson/Jeffries fight	500/100
Corbett vs. Sullivan	750/275
1919 World Series	2,000/650
1932 World Series	800/400
Rose Bowl tickets; all years	100-1,000
Any and all sports tickets from pre-1970	$$$PAID$$$

Film posters advertising prize fights and/or other sports. We will pay a good price depending on the event $100 up

Original fight posters

John vs. Jeffries 1910	$1,000
J.L. Sullivan vs. Corbett	3,000
Dempsey vs. Tunney 1927	600
Any Rocky Marciano	200 up

Sheet music that has a sports theme.
Here are some examples:

Ty Cobb "King of Clubs"	$400
Oh You Jeffries	125
19th cen. baseball sheet music	100-1,000 ea.

Boxing posters wanted. Will pay $500 for this one.

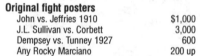

Circa 1930's
football poster. I'll
pay $500 for it!

NEW YORK

Circa 1888
baseball cabinet
photo. Will pay
$750 for these.

We will pay a premium price for a good number of sports related articles that will help us create a bigger and better museum. Try us for friendly service and competitive buying prices. Your pieces, treasured or simply brokered, will arrive at a location where they can be enjoyed by many people of all ages and backgrounds.

We can also arrange a caption for any pieces we buy from an individual, so your name can be attributed to the item in the museum.

Thanks for considering us.

Prices Paid by:	John Buonaguidi	
	540 Reeside Avenue	(800) JIM THORPE
	Monterey, CA 93940	(408) 655-2363

Fishing Tackle

FISHING LURES, REELS & RELATED ITEMS

I'm always buying fishing tackle items pre-1940. I'm a private collector, not a dealer, so I'll pay retail prices for items to go into my collection. I buy single items or complete collections. I use UPS and we can complete our deal within 72 hours, start to finish.

LURES Excellent condition means I pay more. Some company names are Heddon, Shakespeare, Creek Chub Bait Co., South Bend, Pflueger,. Look for glass eyes, multi-colored paint, lots of hooks, spinners and attachments. Metal lures, hollow metal tube type. There are over 10,000 collectable lures all with good value. I like to pay at least $50 each for quality lures, lots more for rare ones.

REELS Pre-1930, bait casting type made of silver, German silver, bronze or black hard rubber or a combo of all of these. Up to 3" in diameter. Names: Meek, Talbot, Milam, Synder, Gayle, etc.

BIG GAME REELS 4" in diameter or larger, used for ocean fishing. Names: E. Vom Hofe, Kovolovsky, Garey, etc.

CATALOGS, FISH PICTURES, CREELS, EMPTY BOXES I like it all, collect it all, and pay you good prices for it.

ALL BAITS PRICED ARE FOR EXCELLENT CONDITION OR BETTER. PRE-1940 BAITS

CREEK CHUB BAIT CO. ("C.C.D.CO")

Pikie minnows	$20-100 ea.
Beetles	20-50 ea.
Wiggle fish	20-50 ea.
Sarasota	100-200 ea.
Close-pin	200 ea.
Ice spearing decoy	500 ea.
Muskey lures	100-300 ea.
Gar minnow	150 ea.
Weed bug	100 ea.

Shakespeare Revolution $150

HEDDON BAIT CO.

Underwater expert	$750 ea.
Slope nose	250 ea.
Muskey minnow	400 ea.
Black sucker	500 ea.
"0" & "00"	200 ea.
100's & 150's	100-200 ea.
Spin diver	200 ea.
Light casting minnow	150 ea.
Crab wigglers	75 ea.
Ice spearing decoy	300-500 ea.
Game fishers	20-50 ea.
Tad polly	40 ea.
Lung frog	50 ea.

Vamps	20-100 ea.
Torpedos	20-75 ea.
Meadow mouse	30 ea.
Flaptails	25-75 ea.
Coast minnows	250 ea.

FRED KEELING BAIT CO.

Muskey experts	$250-500 ea.
Flat experts	150 ea.
Tom Thumb	50 ea.
Muskey Tom	50 ea.
Round experts	100-200 ea.
Surface Tom	50 ea.
Baby Clark expert	150 ea.

MOONLIGHT BAIT CO.

Famous floating bait	$25 ea.
Trout bob	100 ea.
Lady bug wiggler	100-150 ea.
The "Bug"	100 ea.
Dreadnought bait	500 ea.
Fish nipple	25 ea.
Pikaroons	75-150 ea.
#3000 series	100 ea.
Bass seeker	50 ea.

"Heddon" Artistic Minnow $100

PFLUEGER BAIT CO.

Neverfail minnow	$50-150 ea.
Metalized minnow	150 ea.
Trory minnow	500 ea.
Spearing decoy	400 ea.
Pak Ron minnow	250 ea.
Catalina minnow	250 ea.

Wizard minnow	150 ea.
Flying helgramite	2000 ea.
Suprise minnow	100-200 ea.
Kent frog	100-200 ea.
All-In-One	250 ea.
Pal-O-Mine	25-50 ea.
Bender popping minnow	100 ea.
O'Boy minnow	50 ea.
Weedless frog	25-50 ea.
Scoop minnow	20-40 ea.

Bush-Tango Baits	20-150 ea.
Wilson Bait Co.	10-175 ea.

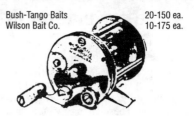

B.F. Meek Reel $250

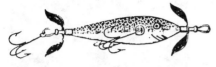

Shakespeare Minnow $100

SHAKESPEARE BAIT CO.
Revolution - wood or cork	$1000 ea.
Revolution hollow metal, aluminum	100-150 ea.
Hydroplane	100 ea.
Punkin-seed minnow	150 ea.
Whilrwind spinner	100 ea.
Muskey minnow	300-500 ea.
Little Joe	50 ea.
Barnacle Bill	100 ea.
Saltwater special	200 ea.
Albany floating bait	500 ea.
Sardina	200 ea.
Favorite floating bait	100 ea.
Evolution minnow	150 ea.
Tarpalunge	100 ea.
Bass-A-Lure	50 ea.
Rhodes mechanical frog	100 ea.
Waukazoo spinner	100 ea.

SOUTH BEND BAIT CO.
Under-water minnows	$50-150 ea.
Lunge-Oreno	100 ea.
Muskie casting minnows	400 ea.
Gulf-Oreno	125 ea.
WhirlOreno	75 ea.
Plunk-Oreno	50 ea.
Vacuum bait	100 ea.
Truck-Oreno	200 ea.
Two-Oreno	50 ea.
Bass-Oreno	10-20 ea.

SMALL BAIT CO "NAMES"
Abbey & Imbrie Co.	$20-100 ea.
Decker Bait Co.	20-100 ea.
Al Foss Bait Co.	10-50 ea.
Jamison Bait Co.	20-75 ea.
Outing Bait Co.	50-100 ea.

REEHS "FRESH WATER"
Billinghurst, "bird cage" style, 3" diameter	$500 ea.
J.A. Coxe, 2" to 4" diameter	50-150 ea.
Heddon, #3-15, 3-25, 3-35, 45, 40	100-300 ea.
B.F. Meek & Sons, #2, 3, 4, 5	100-500 ea.
Meek & Milam, #1, 2, 3, 4, 5	200-600 ea.
Meek (Horton Mfg.)	100-150 ea.
Meisselback, all sizes	50-75 ea.
B.C. Milam, all sizes	150-500 ea.
Orvis fly reel, 1874 patent	500+
Wm. Talbot, "Nevada MD," all sizes	300-700

REELS "SALT WATER"
E. Vom Hofe, size 2" to 8" diameter	$200-100
Kovlovsky, size 3" to 10" diameter	500-1,500
Kline, 3" to 8" diameter	500-100 ea.
Garey, 2" to 6" diameter	303-500 ea.

Pflueger Trory Minnow $500

RODS - FRESH & SALT WATER
Orvis	$100-500 ea.
Phillipson	150-400 ea.
Granger	100-250 ea.
H.L. Leonard	150-500 ea.
Payne	300-1,000 ea.
E.C. Powell	200-500 ea.
Hardy	150-300 ea.
F.E. Thomas	200-500 ea.
Heddon	100-300 ea.

CATALOGS
Pre-1930 - rods, lures, reels, etc.	$25-250 ea.
Creels, the larger the better	25-100 ea.
Empty boxes for:	
Lures	10-100 ea.
Reels	20-100 ea.
Fishing pictures, photos or oils	20-1,000 ea.

I need a photo or xerox photo copy. Group items together. No written info, just clear photos or photo copies.

Prices Paid by: Rick Edmisten	
P.O. Box 686	(818) 763-9406
N. Hollywood, CA 91603	FAX (818) 763-5974
Leave a message. I return all calls.	

Breweriana, Mugs & Other Items

In the 1880's there were over 2400 Breweries in operation in the U.S. With the advent of prohibition in 1919 this number dramatically diminished to 0. In 1933 with the repeal of the great American experiment approximately 1000 Breweries began operation. Today only a handful of major Breweries survive. The advertising items of the pre-prohibition Breweries are the most collectible and therefore the most valuable. These items include, but are not limited to, metal signs, paper signs, glass signs, metal trays, procelain trays, mugs and steins, glasses, calendars, watch fobs, labels, match safes, advertising mirrors, tokens, bottles, openers, post cards. Items from the breweries after 1933 (post-prohibition) include any of the above as well as early beer cans. Beer was put in cans as early as 1935 and cans from 1935-1950 which say Internal Revenue Tax Paid or

Withdrawn from Internal Revenue are the most valuable. Also items with Brewery characters such as the Hamm's bear or Budweisers Bud Man in some cases are valuable. Also round ball type knobs with porcelain or enamel inserts from the Breweries of the 30's and 40's. Also of interest and value are back bar plaster statues.

As is the case with all collectibles, condition is the final criteria in setting value. Rusted, broken, torn and stained have very little value unless it is a one of a kind or extremely rare piece and even then the value is diminished.

A Selection of Steins and Mugs

Anheser-Busch Mettlach Stein showing Adophus Busch	$2,000
Doelger with date of 1916	100
Fairmont with man horseback	75
Muessel 4/10L Mettlach	125
Louis Bergdoll 1849-1893	150
San Antonio Brewing Assn.	150
Glass steins with porcelain inserts in pewter tops	40-150

A Selection of Other Items

Evansville Brewery 1900 calendar with children	$150
Hamm's calendar with pretty girl	350
Kenny Park Brewery calendar with cute little girl	250
Yuengling 1896 calendar with two girls	300
Anheuser-Busch A with eagle watch fob	75-400
Anheuser-Busch match safe	40
Zang sterling silver match safe	100
Anheuser-Busch knife with stanhope	125
Tip trays approx. 4 1/2" round	25-200
Pocket mirrors showing bottle or Brewery	40-150
Brewery china	10-100
Etched glasses	15-100
Labels in old collections or sample books	20-1,000

Post Prohibition Items

Apache Beer Can	$500
Bluebonnet Beer Can	200
Blue Boar Ale Beer Can	250
Eureka Beer Can 3 varieties	100-300
Gold Age Beer Can	400
Indian Queen Ale	1,000
Leidig's	750
Travis	800
Plaster Statue of Grand Prize Pete	$150
Plaster Statue of A-1 Cowboy with clock	300
Ball Tap Knobs	10-100
1930's-40's tin over cardboard signs	10-200
1930's-40's round and square trays	10-200

SPECIAL NOTE – Billy and J.R. beer cans are worth only about 50¢.

Old photos of the inside and outside of Saloons showing Advertising are also wanted, $20-50.

Whiskey advertising prior to prohibition, including tin signs and trays, pretty girls on paper, decorated back bar bottles and mugs.

Photographs of the item are extremely helpful.

Signs (samples of prices paid)

Anheuser-Busch Custers Last Fight 38" x 48" in gold frame	$400
Anheuser-Busch Bottles on Shore (metal or glass)	3,500
Anheuser-Busch Budweiser Girl metal 24"x36"	700
Alamo Girl tin 19"x 25"	1,000
American Brewing Co. glass showing Brewery	850
Burkhardt tin showing man in chair	750
Buffalo tin showing bottles on a table	350
Consumers paper showing goats pulling a wagon	500
Hoster paper showing large Brewery	500
Jetter tin showing Elk and bottle	750
Jung tin showing bottles on table family in background	1,000
Leisy's tin showing men in car with waiter bringing beer	700
Schlitz round tin showing couple in blacksmith shop	500
Zang glass in original gold frame	1,000

Trays (samples of prices paid)

Anheuser-Busch 18"x15" oval showing Brewery	$700
Akron 16" x 14" oval showing Brewery and bottle	500
Berkshire oval showing girl riding horse	450
Breidt oval showing Brewery	750
Buffalo 13" round	300
Dallas 16" oval showing flowers and bottle	400
Foss-Schneider 16" oval showing flags and medals	500
Gerst 12" round showing pretty girl with glass	400
Mathie 12" round large bottle on mule drawn wagon	350
National 16" oval showing cowboys on horseback	1,000
National 12" round showing cowboy breaking through paper	700
Northwestern 12" round showing topless Indian on buffalo	900
Ruhstallers 13" square showing man with ladies in car	500
Stroh 13" square showing Munich child with case	600
Stoll 12" round white porcelain	200

Prices Paid by: Lynn Geyer
300 Trail Ridge
Silver City, NM 88061   (505) 538-2341

Cigar Boxes & Related Items

Since there are 1,500,000 brands of cigars, the brand name means little. Collectors buy most boxes for the pictures on the label. Most boxes are worth from $10 to $30, but a few bring as high as $300+.

Condition is critical in pricing a box. Boxes that are filthy or that have serious writing or water staining on the inside labels are not of interest.

Make certain to contact me with boxes depicting negroes, Chinese, baseball players, cartoon characters, political candidates or claims to cure an ailment.

Left: Revenue stamps before 1910 wraps around box. These are best.
Right: A short 4" tax stamp means your box was made after 1917 and is less likely to be of interest.

Specific Brands, A Selection of

Alcazar box (early style)	$30	Dash little cigars	$50	Lime Kiln Club (rare)	$300
Alcazar tin can	100	Dr. Quack	100	Liver Regulator	80
Asthma Cure	400	Dr. Stork	60	Old Virginia Cheroots	0
Ben Bey (large tin)	10	Eddie Cantor	20	with 1883 tax stamp	20
Bible Class	200	Free Cuba (flag)	40	Our Candidates	50-250
Black Fox tin	100+	Hambone	75	Pittsburgh Smoke (tin)	125
Brown Beauties (tin)	200	Health brand box	75	Rail Splitter (either)	75
Brown Beauties (box)	20	Health Brand (tin & paper)	30	Rochester Rod & Gun	45
Buster Brown box	125-250	Health Brand (litho on tin)	75	Sam Gompers	30
Buster Brown (tin)	750	Hoffman House (naked)	75	Temptation	125
Capadura	35	Hoffman House (clothed)	10	Thora (semi-nude)	30
Cheese It (round)	250	Home Run stogies	500+	Three Jackasses	75
Cure all	80	KKKK	300	White Cap ("get out")	350
Dan Patch (wood box)	50	Lime Kiln Club (common)	125	Women's Rights	350

Brands in Wooden Boxes Worth $1 or Less

44	Dime Bank	Juan de Fuca	Reynaldo
1886	Dixie Maid	King Edward	RG Dun
7-20-4	Donalda	La Corona	Robt. Burns
Admiration	Dunhill	La Fendrich	Roberts
Alhambra	Dutch Masters	La Palina	Roi Tan
Antonio y Cleopatra	El Producto	La Primadora	Rum Soaked
Aurelia	El Sidelo	La Yerba	San Felice
Back & Co.	El Trellis	Little Fendrich	Sano
Bances	El Verso	London Whiffs	Santa Fe
Bayuk Ribbon	Emanello	Lovera	Spencer Morris
Belinda	Factory Seconds	M. & O.	Swann
Benson & Hedges	Factory Smokers	M.Ibold	Swisher Sweets
Bering	FactoryThrowouts	Mark IV	Tampa Nugget
Bock y Ca.	Garcia Grande	Marsh Wheeling	Te Amo
Bold	Garcia, Jr.	Monogram	Thompson & Co.
Brooks & Co.	Garcia y Vega	Muniemaker	Tiona
Chancellor	Gold Label	Muriel	Tom Keene
Chas Denby	Habanello	Optimo	Top Stone
Charles Thomson	Hav-A-Tampa	Owl (most)	Tudor Arms
Cinco	Havana Ribbon	Partagas	Tufuma
Corina	Have A Sweet	Perfecto Garcia	Van Dyke
Cremo	House of Windsor	Phillies	Y-B
Cuesta Rey	Humo	Pippens	Webster
Cuesto	H.Upmann	Ramon Allones	White Owl
Del Cara	John Ruskin	Red Dot	Wolf. Bros.

**Boxes after 1945 have no value, except very unusual ones.
Foreign boxes except Canadian, almost never have value.
Cuban boxes made after 1900 are worth $1 or less; earlier $10.**

Boxes with These Labels are Wanted

Famous Indian chiefs	$40-75	Political candidates	$30-250
Other Indians	20-50	KKK themes	200+
Cowboys, generic	20-100	Cartoon characters	30-300
Famous badmen	40-100	Winnie Winkle	10
Buffalo Bill	150	Yellow Kid (color)	200
Movie cowboys	30-100	Buster Brown	125-250
Movie stars	30-100	Mutt & Jeff	50
Negro racism	60-300	Maggie & Jiggs	150
Chinese racism	75-300	Gambling, high life	10-40
Baseball	75-100+	Bicycle riding	30-50
Joe Tinker	150	Puns and jokes	20-50+
Cy Young	500+	Weddings	30+
Other named players	100+	Uncle Sam	20-50+
Other sports	30-100	Men at work	20-50
Race horses, specific	30-75	Women in "men's" occupations	30-75
Fishing	20-40	Fairs & Expos	30-100
Boxing	50-150	Special events	30-100
Railroad trains	20-60	Policemen	20-50
Overland (early)	10	Firemen	30-75
Overland (snowbound train)	75	Other civil servants	20-50
Christmas	10-30	Children smoking	30-50
Santa Claus	50-100	Religious figures	20-40
Other holidays	30-75	Women's rights, voting	75-175
Nudes	30-100	Animals doing human things	20-40
Risque (naughty)	100-200	Maps of cities, counties, etc.	20-50
XXX rated	500	Presidents of the U.S.	20-100+

Other Styles of Boxes Wanted

- Book shaped boxes are $10-20, but great labels can make them $100 up.
- Boxes in unusual shapes like mailboxes, railroad cars, game boards, bottles, and the like will usually bring from $50-$150.
- Large floor standing chests are worth from $300 to $700 or more.
- Glass jars are wanted, but only with unusual or interesting labels, $40 up.
- Tin cans, valued between $15 and $500. Near mint condition only.

Other Items Related to Cigars

Label catalogs: value ranges from $20 to as much as $1,000 or more, depending on the printer, number of labels, age, and subject matter.

Photos of factories and stores: photos bring from $20 to $40 with a few bringing more, depending on subject matter. Want interiors, exteriors, salesmen, delivery wagons, box factories, lithographers, etc.

Books listing factories and addresses: Trade directories from 1860 to 1930 will bring $100 each. 1887 and a few others will bring more.

Cigar band collections are not of interest. Other buyers are available.

Musical instruments made from cigar boxes: Value ranges from $50 to $150 depending on the workmanship, condition, and style.

Other items made from boxes will be considered.

Paintings of cigar boxes: Value is $200 up, with most under $700.

Prices Paid by: Tony Hyman
Box 3000
Pismo Beach, CA 93448 (805) 773-6777

Make a Xerox™ copy of the inside lid of a box you wish to sell. It is helpful if you also include a Xerox™ of the top and bottom. It is not necessary to copy the sides. If the box is full of cigars, don't disturb them. Copy the outside end that has a pictorial label. If the box is an unusual shape, take a photograph. All mail answered if you include an SASE. *Handbook of American Cigar Boxes,* a 176p hardcover book that teaches you how to evaluate boxes, complete with up to date price guide is available for only $17.95.

Cigarette Lighters
FIRE MAKING DEVICES, RELATED ITEMS & INFORMATION
Lighters have been associated with tobacco for more than three centuries. Making fire goes back further than can be imagined. The history of these subjects and the contrivances that have been conceived are of interest to me.

Prices determined by desirability, age, scarcity & condition
A gold Dunhill watch lighter of the highest grade in the poorest condition has little value more than its content of gold. Brand new in the box with instructions, this lighter may be worth several thousands of dollars. On the other hand, a 17th century flintlock tinderbox in any condition may also be quite valuable provided it is one of only a couple examples known to exist. Generally speaking, modern lighters are effected most by dings, scratches and other wear that comes from use and whether it is complete or missing parts, etc. Call me if you have any questions about lighters.

Call me collect if you have:

Any Dunhill lighters in gold or silver,		Column	$1,000+
with watches especially. Dunhill Hidden		Jet	300+
watch in gold	$3,000+	Ruler	200+
		Bell	300+
Other Dunhills include:		Roman Lamp	300+
The Book Lighter	300+	Ball in sterling or gold	300+
The Hunting Horn	400+	Silent Flames	30-1,000
Tintrol	1,000+	Aquariums	500+

- Table and pocket lighters, except rectangular pocket lighters made during the 1950's and later unless they have a watch or other special feature built in

- Roll-A-Lite models are worth a little more than the gold content to me

- Any other gold, silver or enamel lighters of quality: Clark, Eterna, Van Cleef and Arpells, Boucheron, Cartier, Tiffany, Asprey (models that were made during the 1920's, 30's and 40's)   I pay to $5,000 for the right lighter

- Ronson lighters in the form of animals and other figural table lighters. Also, incense burners, bookends, inkwells marked A.M.W. art metal works or L.V.A. $50-1,000

- Pre-1900 lighters or devices for making fire are my favorite

- Unusual figural lighters of artistic appeal made during the first half of the 20th century or before

- Art deco designs, whether pocket or table models, uncommon Evans, Elgin American, Lincoln, Kum-A-Part, Myon, Hermes, Lancel, Transfo, brass trench lighters, Parker, Beney, McMurdo, Bruma, Thorens, Golden Wheel, Swank, Abdulla, Austrian Spelter, Ronson figural, occupied Japan

- Zippos with square corners or the hinge soldered to the outside of the case

- Zippos with Disney characters, political and tobacco ads

- Cigarette case and lighter combinations in near to mint condition are wanted, especially those with watches and compact made by Ronson, Dunhill Marathon, Evans and other companies $20-3,000

- Any books, catalogs, photos or people using anything depicting making fire, sparks, friction, advertisements, ads or items such as punch boards, etc. $10-500

For brands and models not listed please inquire. Lighters may not necessarily have a brand name or markings to be of interest to me. Photos are most helpful when asking for specific information. Entire collections may be of interest for purchase.

- I will say that no one will pay higher prices than myself for the things that I don't have.

- Items from the 17th, 18th and 19th centuries; I seek any items that I don't have.

- Items with flint and tinder

- Chemical bottles with mechanical devices attached to them

- Early matches from the mid to beginning of the 19th century

- Devices that used caps or gun powder

- Solar devices whether pocket or table models $20-10,000 for the best of this category (see photo)

Verbal appraisals of single pieces and entire collections are available for a reasonable fee. Twenty two years experience and continuing.

Prices Paid by: Tom O'Key
Send self addressed, stamped envelope to:
P.O. Box 504, Anaheim, CA 92815   (714) 630-8919
Please include your phone number.   FAX (714) 632-8275

Cowboy Collectibles

Ranch gear, rodeo, movie, vaquero and wild west shows can all be considered Cowboy Collectables. The price ranges given are to be applied to items in good condition with original parts and from before WWII (1940s). Outstanding examples will go beyond these prices in certain markets. We stay flexible and approachable. Although the best is sought, everything is considered.

Boots, Early, pre 1940s with color	$40-100
Buckle Sets, Silver Ranger Sets	35-75
Cuffs, Leather, Maker marked	85-200
Cuffs, Leather, Unmarked	40-100
Gauntletts, Maker marked	50-100
Hats, Big 5" Brim, worn	40-80
Hats, J.B. Stetsons pre 1930	40-200
Photos, Working Cowboy & Studio	15-35
Scarves, Silk with Cowboy Scene	20-50

Chaps, Leather, unmarked	$85-350
Chaps, Leather, maker marked	200-500
Chaps, Decorated with Conchas	500-1,000
Chaps, "Woolie", good condition	400-1,000
Reatas, Braided rawhide	75-200
Reins, Braided rawhide	75-200

Saddles, Sterling Silver mounted with marks	
e.g. Bohlin, Visalia:	$1,000
Military Saddles	100-200
Saddle Company Catalogues pre-1940	
Names to look for are: Bohlin, Coggshall,	
R.T. Frazier, Furstnow, S.C. Gallup,	
Hamley Heiser, Main & Winchester,	
Padgett Brothers, Porter, Visalia & others	

Holster and Gun Belts Maker marked, old	
No guns however!!	$75-500

Horsehair Work: Hitched & braided-old	
Bridles with reins & complete	$200-2,000
Belts with Buckles	30-200
Hat Bands (not new from Mexico)	20-100
Quirts, Multi-colored	50-350

Spurs

Names to look for Anchor marked, J.O. Bass, Crocket, G.S. Garcia, Kelly Bros., McChesney, Ricardo, Star Marked No Far East Imports Please!

Spurs, plain iron, pre-1930's	$75-200
Spurs, Silver Mounted	100-1,000
Old Mexican Silver Mounted Spurs	50-200
Spur Straps, old leather	15-50
Spur Straps, Maker Marked	50-100

$350

$650

$350

$175

Horse Bits

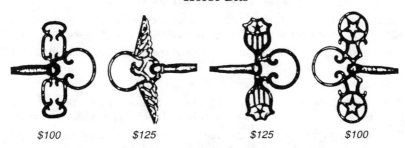

$100 $125 $125 $100

Bits, Silver Mounted Riding Bridle Bits $100-1,000
Bits, Old Iron, driving & riding   5-30
Bits, U.S. Military, pre 1900   75-500
Bits, Fancy Driving-Intricate checks   25-125

Tin Tags

TOBACCO TIN TAG TRADING CENTER USA
sTagger Lee Jacobs
P.O. Box 3098
Colorado Springs, CO 80934
(719) 473-7101

Collections purchased. Criteria for bidding is condition, color, age, subject and rarity.
Small collections under 500 tags, receive less per tag than large collections over
1000 tags. This is because large collections likely have rare and unusual tags in them.
Small collections $1 or less per tag
Large collections   up to $4 per tag
Individual tags – Blacks, political, war related, ladies & Sport tags bring
premium prices   50¢-$75

Individual Example of Rare Tags

Slide Kelly Slide (Baseball)	$60-80
Saturday Night (Nudes)	75-100
Cosby's Hambone (Black)	35-60
War Cry (War)	25-30

$15 $15 $10 $20

McChesney Bits & Spurs
New Reference Book with price guide and many detailed photos.

Prices Paid by: Lee Jacobs
P.O. Box 3098
Colorado Springs, CO 80934   (719) 473-7101

Indian Artifacts

- **Stone Items** - arrowheads, spearheads, stone axes, celts, pipes, ceremonial pieces, gorgets, bannerstones, budstones. Will pay up to $2000 for good budstones or 1 item.

- **Baskets** - Apache, California, Pomo, Northwest coast, Puma, Eskimo, etc. Basket must be in good condition. Will pay up to $2000 for 1 basket.

- **Weavings** - Navaho, Satillo Serapes. Will pay up to $2000.

- **Bone, Shell & Wood** - Eskimos, Northwest coast, awls, Effigy, wood carvings, rattles, bone or ivory, boxes, wood masks or items. Will pay up to $2000 for items.

- **Beadwork** - Awl bags, possible bags, knife sheaths, bandolier bags, dolls, pipe bags, mirror cases. Any type of beadwork. Will pay up to $2000 for one item.

- **Pipe Tomahawks** - Cast iron or brass tomahawk heads. Prefer with original handles. Knife blades, staffs. Will pay up to $2000 for one item.

- **Pottery** - Acoma, Hopi, Pueblo, Zia, Zuni. Will pay up to $2000 for one item.

Arrowpoints and knives are evaluated on size, workmanship, material, attractiveness and authenticity.

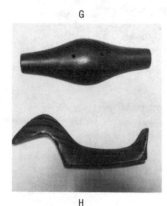

(A) Drill points, Midwestern US, 300 AD to 1500 AD Eight illustrated — 20-200
(B) Archaic Thebes point, 200 BC to 500 AD, 4" long — 100
Longer lengths can go to — 1500
(C) Hardin barb, Mississippi River, 100 BC to 500 AD 4" long — 100
Longer lengths can go to — 1000
(D) Big knife, Mississippi River, 1000 BC to 1200 AD. One of the desirable shapes — 100
Other configurations can bring — 500 up

(E) Dixon points, Illinois, 1000 BC to 1000 AD — 100
(F) Dalton, Mississippi River, 8000 BC to 6000 BC (also called "early man" or "paleo points") at 3" long brings — 100
(G) Hopewell corner notch, Illinois, 1000 BC to 500 AD — 100
Longer lengths can go to — 1000
(H) Birdstone, Midwest, 4000 BC to 1000 BC — 1000
(I) Pipe tomahawks, circa 1800's, must have original head & handle — up to 1000

   I am only interested in items that have been obtained legally and not off of any state or federal lands, national forests or from any other areas deemed protected and which it is illegal to remove Indian artifacts.

   Please feel free to call or list what you have and make a drawing, xerox or send a picture giving all measurements. Include your home and work phone numbers.

Prices Paid by:	Jan Sorgenfrei 10040 St. Rt. 224 West Findlay, OH 45840	Days (419) 422-8531 FAX (419) 422-5321

Antique Bottles

Thousands of products were sold in bottles during the 19th century. Many of those bottles are collectible today, whether they held food, medicine, soda, alcoholic beverages, cologne, or ink. Such bottles may sell for as little as $1, but many can be worth hundreds or possibly thousands of dollars. A full description is essential. I will make offers to private parties, but dealers are expected to price the items they offer.

Bottles after 1920, often with threaded caps, have little value. Plain, unembossed bottles have very little value, especially if they are clear in color.

BOTTLES OF THESE TYPES ARE WANTED - PRE-1920

USA Hospital Dept bottles	$75-300	Poisons in cobalt blue, dark green,	
Bitters in all colors and shapes	25-500	and amber with embossed designs	
Flasks with embossed pictures (eagles,		or skull and crossbones, may be round,	
portraits, flags, trains, patriotic		square, or multi-sided	$25-250
symbols) or fancy designs	50-500	Cures	25-100
Barber bottles in fancy colors, shapes,		Liquors with embossed names and	
or with enamel decorations	50-200	pictures, in nice colors, may be	
Inks in colors with multiple sides or		cylinders, squares, or flask shaped	50-250
in cone or teakettle shapes	50-200	Early free-blown bottles and flasks	50-250
Figurals in glass or German porcelain		Miniatures and samples of any	
in shapes of people, animals, etc.	25-250	bottled product	25-150
Fire grenades in bright colors and		Stoneware jugs with interesting	
unusual shapes	50-250	product names, especially bitters	75-350
Patent medicines with odd names,		Shaker medicine bottles	25-50
embossed pictures, pontil scars,		Colorful cologne and perfume bottles,	
colorful labels	25-150	especially with colorful labels	25-50
Sodas in colors, with "blob" type lips,		Food bottles with cathedral-style	
embossed names and pictures	20-100	embossed sides	50-300
Bar decanters with colored enamel brand		Product jars (gum, candy, pills)	
names or pictures upon them	35-200	with embossed names and	
Fruit jars with odd names, embossed		glass or tin lids	75-200
pictures, odd colors	25-300		

BOTTLE-RELATED ITEMS WANTED - PRE-1920

Trays and tip trays with colorful scenes		Pocket mirrors advertising bottled	
and featuring ads for bottled products	$75-500	and other products	$25-100
Signs of tin, wood, or glass with colorful		Early photos of glass companies,	
scenes and featuring ads for bottled		breweries, saloons, beer wagons,	
products	100-1,000	patent medicine shows	10-50
Posters of paper or cardboard with		Pocket match safes advertising bottled	
colorful scenes and featuring ads		and other products	25-75
for bottled products	50-400	Pocket knives advertising bottled products	25-75
Etched or embossed glasses or shot		Glass whimsies such as canes, chains,	
glasses with ads for beer, whiskey,		and gavels	75-200
or bitters	25-200		
Mugs or steins with ads for bottled			
products	50-250		
Sales catalogs from glass companies,			
label printing companies, drug and			
saloon supply companies, liquor and			
beer suppliers	25-200		
Wall match holders advertising bottled			
and other products	75-250		
Trade cards advertising bottled products	5-25		
Pin back buttons advertising bottled			
and other products	10-35		

Early patent medicines "Gargling Oil" & "Patent 1859" $25-$150+. Inks in good colors $50-$200+. Flasks with Embossed pictures $50-$500+. Bottles with cathedral style designs $5-$300+. Color is prime factor for value.

Prices Paid by: Steve Ketcham
Box 24114
Minneapolis, MN 55424   (612) 920-4205

Accurate descriptions of condition are very important. Mention damage such as chips or cracks on bottles or rust and paint loss on tin advertising. Include also size, color, and details of embossing or wording. A photocopy of any label is helpful. Return privilege, please.

Boy Scout Patches

Since the beginning of the Boy Scouts of America in 1910, scouts of all ages have collected scouting memorabilia. Over the years, the primary focus has shifted from the acquisition of entire uniforms from scouts of other countries to the collecting of primarily U.S. patches, medals and neckerchiefs. The area of strongest interest, and therefore value, is Order of the Arrow. These patches almost always have 3 "W"'s (WWW) and the number of the lodge. The Order of the Arrow is an honor brotherhood in scouting founded in 1915 and early items of memorabilia are much sought after. Even more recent O.A. patches bring 2.50 each compared to pennies for less collected local events such as camporees and scout-o-ramas. Prices quoted are always for mint, unused patches. A good, used patch will usually bring 50% of the price for a new one. I prefer to buy entire collections and accumulations, but will of course buy individual patches I need. Patches I need go into a display which you might see one day at a scouting event. Patches I already have or cannot fit into my collection, usually find their way into the collections of other scouters across the country. Following is a listing of SOME of the items I buy:

- **ORDER OF THE ARROW** patches all years - the older the better
  Example: Lodges 155 Michikinaqua, 219 Calusa, 246 Wakoda, Ma Ta
  Cam Round and 538 Baluga Lodge - $1,000 ea. Lodges 47 Hanigus,
  154 Checote, 177 Victorio, 543 Monsey, 311 Koo Ben Sho, 182
  Lone Wolf, 370 Massassoit - $500 ea. Any Order of the Arrow
  lodge patch $2.50 ea.

- **NATIONAL JAMBOREE** staff items and armbands – the older the better.
  Example: 1953 and 1957 O.A. Service Troop Armbands - $500 ea. 1953
  Jamboree staff jacket patch with "California" below wagon - $300

- **WORLD JAMBOREE** items - the older the better.
  Example: 1924 World Jamboree flag shaped serially numbered official
  silk patch – $2,000 ea. 1933, 1937, and 1947 World Jamboree
  official patches - $250 ea.

- **BSA MEDALS AND AWARDS** pre-1950
  Example: First Honor Medal in Gold - $1,000

- **RANKS AND INSIGNIA** pre-1940
  Example: Original Eagle Medals 1912-15 with the Eagle made of
  Bronze or Brass - $1,000 ea. Ranger Medal $300, Ace Medal $500.

- **WORLDS FAIR SERVICE CORPS** pre-1964
  Example: 1933 Worlds Fair Service Corps patch or neckerchief: 150 ea.

- **BADGES AND COLLAR PINS OF OFFICE**, especially national level
  Example: First International Commissioner patch $500 ea. First
  National Scout Commissioner patch $250 ea.

- **NATIONAL ORDER OF THE ARROW CONFERENCE** memorabilia
  Example: 1927 Wallet $500, 1927 Celluloid Pin $1,000, 1933 Celluloid Pin $1,000, 1936 Leader Ribbon $400, 1940 Medal with ribbon and name bar $500, 1940 Staff Neckerchief $400, 1975 armbands $50 ea.

- **OA NATIONAL COMMITTEE** official items
  Example: Red felt vigil sash for committee members $2,000. Red cloth sash issued for 75th Ann of OA $500.

- **FELT ORDER OF THE ARROW SASHES**
  Example: Original white arrow on black felt $750. Red on white felt VIGIL sash with triangle in center of the arrow $250.

- **NATIONAL ORDER OF THE ARROW CONFERENCE CONTINGENT ISSUES**
  Example: Neckerchiefs issued by lodges for their contingent to the NOAC $10 ea. Beaded flaps issued for NOAC's $50 ea. Many other contingent pieces have a strong premium.

- **CHENILLE OA PATCHES**
  Example: These are patches made like High School letters with the wool raised loops sometimes called "rugs". Any chenille is worth $20. An original from Packanke or Eriez Lodges is worth $500.

- **REGION PATCHES**
  Example: patches from the original 12 Regions are only worth $3-5 ea. This is the biggest change in value and surprise for the "old-timers". Since the change in regions (now to only 4), the value has been lost. Still valuable however are the early felt Region patches: R5-$100, R8-$200, R9-$100, R12-$100

- **PHILTURN ROCKY MOUNTAIN SCOUT CAMP**
  Example: patches (originals) $200 ea.

- **COUNCIL SHOULDER PATCHES (CSP'S)**
  Example: Kootaga reverse colors, Nevada purple dollar, Washington Trails fleur de lis, Okefenokee "stars and bars" $500 ea. Any CSP 75¢ ea. in quantity.

- **PATROL MEDALLIONS**
  Example: Round without "B.S.A." $20 ea. Square $75 ea.

- **MERIT BADGES**
  Example: Old square merit badges $6 ea. MINT and $2 ea. used.

- **CAMP PATCHES**
  Example: Pre-1960 cloth - $1 ea. felt - $2 ea.

- **CAMPOREES, SCOUT-O-RAMAS, SCOUT CIRCUS AND OTHER LOCAL ISSUES**
  These essentially have no value except in the town that issued them and even then they sell for a very small amount.

The very best way to show me what you have is to xerox the patches. You can usually get 8-10 patches on a page. From a xerox (black and white is fine) I can tell what issues you have, the condition of the patches and be better able to discuss prices. with you. In advance, I'd like to thank you for any help that you can give me.

Prices Paid by:	Dr. Ronald G. Aldridge	Work (214) 351-3490 Ext. 3107
	250 Canyon Oaks Drive	Home (817) 455-2519
	Argyle, TX 76226	FAX (817) 455-5094

Marine Artifacts

The following categories are too subjective and complicated to reduce to average price ranges. Each of your items must be considered on a per item basis. It is impossible to accurately estimate range without seeing an item in person. Items range from $100 to more than $10,000. This page is to inform you of items which are more readily sellable and to offer my services when you are ready.

SCRIMSHAW

Scrimshaw is work done by whalemen during the era of whaling, perhaps including the work of retired or shorebound whalemen. We are only interested in 19th century antique items. We are particularly interested in American, Australian, English and Dutch material. We do not buy contemporary work, reproductions, or items of questionable age. Items to look for:

Sperm whale teeth decorated with whaling or other types of scenes
Whalebone furniture, pie crimper or jagging wheels
Swifts or yarn winders, and other tools, toys or household implements
Inlaid boxes

HALF HULL MODELS

Before blueprints sectional, scale models were constructed as practical guides for the lofting and building of ships. Since both sides of a ship are the same only a half was made. Some were later painted or mounted and given to owners or used as designs. We are interested in original pieces, primarily American but also British in the following categories:

Identified or anonymous American clippers, merchant vessels, whaleships and yachts
Steam ships in mirrored glass cases

We are interested in memorabilia in the following categories:

NAVIGATIONAL INSTRUMENTS: backstaff, sextants and octants pre-1900

GLOBES ON STANDS: pre-1900

TELESCOPES: tripod mounted, multi-sided, presentation or unusual

U.S. LIFE SAVING & LIGHTHOUSE SERVICE MEMORABILIA: medals, life-guns, clocks, logs, buttons, uniforms, photos, virtually all.

MARINE CLOCKS: striking, Chelsea & Howard 10" diameter or large, presentations, but virtually all. Seth Thomas with outside strikers only.

MARINE PAINTINGS: American mostly 19th century, but some 20th, by the usual group of Bradford, Buttersworth, Drew, Gifford, Jacobsen, Lane, & Salmon. We both buy and broker important works with discretion.

MARINE CHINA: Boston mails, steamship & ocean line, yacht & yacht club, commemorative American clippers & yachting.

AMERICA'S CUP MEMORABILIA: especially "J" boats from the 1930's as well as anything pre-1910.

ALL YACHTING MEMORABILIA both sail & power

ANYTHING PERTAINING TO NANTUCKET including Nantucket baskets

SHIP MODELS

We are interested in the following types of ship models in almost any condition. Since we restore them, broken models are a plus as damage during shipment is less a problem.

Except in extraordinary circumstances we do not want: Spanish galleons, Chinese junks, the Mayflower, Viking ships, Mississippi riverboats, anything in plastic or fiberglass.

We are seeking 18th, 19th and early 20th century models of quality, especially planked models in original paint and decoration.

WANTED

American clipper ships identified or anonymous: 19th flying fish, fine condition $1500 20th century Flying Cloud good condition, $350; Great Republic 19th century kit $100

Whaleships American or other including contemporary factory ships as well as whaleboats, particularly in bone. Wanderer, early 20th century, sailor made $850; Morgan early 20th century $550; Alice Mandel 19th century planked $1500; Azorian Whaleboat, 20th century bone $700.; Whaleboat late 19th-early 20th century bone $1000

Yacht Models both sail and power. Foam 19th century schooner yacht $1500; Cutter circa 1885 $500; Topsail sloop circa 1885 $650; wrecked sloop circa 1880 $175; cabin cruiser circa 1930 $400;

America's Cup Defenders & Challengers America 19th century $850; America 20th century kit wrecked $150; Volunteer 19th century $1000; Columbia 19th century wrecked $450

Steam Yachts unidentified circa 1910 $750; unidentified wreck circa 1890 $500

Sidewheel Steamers Portland 20th century kit $450; Nantasket 19th century fine planked $2000; unidentified wreck $250

Actual Sailing Models Marblehead class circa 1930 mahogany planked $850; sloop circa 1880 $950; sloop circa 1938 planked $650; wreck circa 1930 $250; wreck circa 1900 $175; wreck circa 1940 $75

Merchant Sailing Ships 19th century American ship planked $1200; 19th century American ship solid hull $450; early 20th century kit $350; 19th century wreck $150; 20th century wreck $100

LOG BOOKS & JOURNALS

Particularly American, but whaling items of any nationality. Condition is important along with illustrations, whalestamps and incidents in the voyage. Boring, routine trips are less interesting.

WE HAVE PURCHASED THE FOLLOWING IN THE PAST YEAR:

Log Book Helen Augusta of Newport 1850-1854. Complete voyage to the Arctic $2000
Log Book Ship Louisiana of New Bedford 1853-1857. Complete voyage to the Pacific $2200
Log Book Black Eagle of New Bedford 1866-1867. Complete voyage to Hudson's Bay $500
Log Book Rosewell King of New London 1880-1881. Sea-elephant voyage to Desolation Island $500
Log Book John R. Manta of New Bedford 1908-1910. Partial journal in the Atlantic, along with 4 shipboard account books for other whalers $650
Ship's Papers of the Bark Anaconda of New Bedford 1856-1860 with papers from the schooner George Brown of Boston 1866-1868. $250

We buy complete marine librarys of out of print books in good or better shape. Condition is essential.
•U.S. Merchant Ship Lists 1867-1915 Up to $100 for pre-1880 lists, $35-50 pre-1890;
   $25-40 pre-1900; $15-20 to 1915
•U.S. Life Saving Service Annual Lists All Years. Up to $75 pre-1900; Up to $50 pre-1920;
   Up to $35 pre-1940; Up to $25 other
•U. S. Lighthouse Service Reports. All years same price structure as Life Saving Service.
•New York Harbor Shipping Records All Years Pre-1900. Up to $200 pre-1867;
   Up to $100 pre-1880; Up to $75 pre-1890; Up to $50 pre-1900.
•Lloyd's Registers of U.S. shipping all pre-1900. Same price structure as U.S. merchant ship lists.
•Lloyd's Register of American Yachts All Pre-1940. Up to $50 pre-1900;
   Up to $30 pre-1915; Up to $25 pre-1940.
•Mannings Yacht Lists Pre-1910. Up to $50.
•Yachtsman's Annuals with Half-Tone Photos by Stebbins, Peabody & Jackson. Up to $50.
•Instantaneous Marine Views David Mason Little 1882. UP to $500
•Mott's American & English Yachts 2 volumes. Up to $550.
•Representative American Yachts by Henry Peabody. Up to $450
•Yacht Portraits by N.L. Stebbins. Up to $250.

We aggressively purchase both American & British marine photography. Bound volumes of America's Cup Races pre-WWI are of particular interest. Also photos 14" x 18" and larger. We will pay exceptional prices for exceptional images. Good or better condition is essential.

David Mason Little		Up to $100 per image
Henry Peabody	Up to $50 for 8 x 10	Up to 500 for large images
N.L. Stebbins	Up to 50 for 8 x 10	Up to 500 for large images
W.B. Jackson	Up to 50 for 8 x 10	Up to 500 for large images
Lincoln	Up to 50 for 8 x 10	Up to 500 for large images
Levick	Up to 50 for 8 x 10	Up to 250 for large images
C. E. Bolles	Up to 50 for 8 x 10	Up to 250 for large images
Burton	Up to 50 for 8 x 10	Up to 250 for large images
Rosenfeld	Up to 50 for 8 x 10	Up to 250 for large images
West & Son Swansea	Up to 50 for 8 x 10	Up to 250 for large images
Bekens of Cowes	Up to 50 for 8 x 10	Up to 250 for large images
Early Image of Divers & Their Equipment		Up to 250

SIGNED OR UNSIGNED IMAGES OF THE FOLLOWING:

American Harbor Scenes Boston, N.Y., San Francisco, Newport
Nantucket, Whaling, Yachts (sail, steam & power), Schooners, Occupational: sailmakers, fishermen, identified captains, launchings, shipbuilding, sailing craft with more than 3 masts, grand banks fishing schooners, unusual small craft.

We do not buy naval material after 1900.

Prices Paid by: Andrew Jacobson
Marine Antiques
Box 2155
S. Hamilton, MA 01982   (508) 468-6276

Typewriters & Calculators

Collectible models range in price from $50 to $4,000. Price depends on 1) rarity, 2) desirability and 3) condition. Prices listed here are for machines in "very good" condition. Please expect lower prices for lesser condition. Due to the huge number of typewriter brands, this list is only partial. It's always best to send a photo if you want an accurate price quote. Note: "index" refers to machines without keyboards.

Brooks typewriter, $2,000

TYPEWRITERS

American (kebyd or index)	$100	Jackson	$1,000
Bar-Lock (ornate)	300	Lambert	350
Bennett	50	Merritt	200
Boston	2,000	Mignon	75
Brooks	2,000	Munson	300
Caligraph #1 (caps only)	1,000	National (curved keyboard)	350
Caligraph #2, 3, 4	100	Odell	200
Chicago	150	Remington No. 2,3	150
Chicago No. 3	400	Remington No. 4 (all caps)	450
Columbia Bar Lock	100	Sholes & Glidden (black)	1,000
Columbia (index)	500	Sholes & Glidden (ornate)	2,500
Commercial Visible	350	Sholes & Glidden (treadle)	4,000
Corona (folding, black)	30	Ford	1,000
Corona (folding, colors)	50	International (keyboard)	500
Crown (index)	500	International (index)	250
Daugherty	275	McCool	500
Densmore	100	Niagara	500
Edison	1,000	Oliver No. 1 (nickel base)	1,000
Emerson	200	Oliver No. 2 (nickel base)	125
Automatic (brass)	1,000	Oliver No. 2, 3 (green base)	50
Blickensderfer Electric	3,000	Rapid (Dayton, OH)	500
Blickensderfer (any other)	65	Sampo (index)	500
Fitch	1,000	Saturn	1,000
Fox	75	Sterling	500
Gardner	1,000	Victor (index)	500
Hall	175	Wagner	300
Hammond No. 1	350	Wellington	50
Hammond (all others)	65	Williams	250
Hammonia	1,500	World	200

CALCULATORS:

Addi	$65	Grant	$3,000
Addo	200	Grossbeck's	100
Adix	250	Jeffers	150
Alpina	300	Kuhrt	50
Austria	150	Kuli	600
Baldwin	5,000	Locke Adder	100
Berggens	350	Lord's	500
Bri-Cal	50	Madas (1908)	200
Brunsviga	40	Millionaire	350
Buettner	4,000	Millionaire (wood)	1,000
Bunzel-Delton	400	Mercedes Euklid #1	200
Burkhardt	700	Marcedes Euklid #8	150
Calculagraph	50	Monopol	1,000
Calcumeter	75	Multifix	100
Comptometer	40	Original Ohdner #1	1,000
Comptometer		Payen Arithmometer	1,000
(wood only)	150	Peerless	150
Consul the Educated		Quixsum Mod. C	100
Monkey	75	Rapid	50
Conto	150	Saxonia	150
Curta	85	Scribiola	100
Dactyle	50	Smallwood	1,000
Denominator	50	Spalding	700
Diera	250	Thomas Arithmometer	1,000
DTA	500	TIM	150
Duco	100	Triumph	500
Fowler's	30	Universal (J. Bamberger)	500
Golden Gem	20	Webb's adder	150
Graeber's Arithmometer	2,000	XxX	500

RELATED ITEMS

Ribbon tins: vast majority are about $3 each. Oldest and rarest are up to $30.
Trade literature: magazines about the typewriter industry, or any pre-1900 magazines with "Phonograph" or "Phonographic" in the titles (phonographic was the old word for "stenographic" and had nothing to do with record players!). Pay $5-15 each.

Catalogs: office equipment catalogs pre-dating 1910. Pay $25-200

Typewriters or calculators with little or no collectors value:

Burroughs	Remington No. 10 or above
Corona	Royal (except gold-plate trim)
L.C. Smith	Smith-Corona
Monarch	(except sterling silver)
Monroe	Underwood
Oliver No. 5 or above	Woodstock

Prices Paid by: Darryl Rehr
2591 Military Ave.
Los Angeles, CA 90064
(310) 477-5229

Guns & Trapping

GUN RELATED:

Item	Average Price	Maximum Price
Calendars & posters	$350-500	$4,000
Shotshell boxes (cardboard)	35-50	3,000
Catalogs & pamphlets	20-50	1,000
Gunpowder cans	20-75	1,500
Glass target balls	75-150	5,000
Glass ball throwers	300-1,000	1,500
Pin back buttons	20-75	500
Gun advertising envelopes	30-60	400
.22 boxes	10-30	1,000
Etc. (too many to list)		

All items must be original, pre-1940, from the manufacturer, in 80% or better condition and complete. I do not buy NRA items, hardware store or sporting goods store catalogs or repros. Small unusual companies are generally more desirable then larger, commonly known ones. Examples of good companies are Robin Hood, American Ammunition, California Powder Works, Dixie, house brands (hand loads), Parker.

Multicolored scene on empty 12 gauge shotshell box from CA Powder Works. $2000

TRAPPING RELATED ITEMS:

Item	Average Price	Maximum Price
Steel traps	$10-200	$2,500
Trap catalogs	25-100	200
Fur company catalogs	10-25	35
Tips To Trappers (Sears Roebuck)	10-15	25
Lure bottles & shipping containers	10-25	40
Calendars	75-100	150
Animal trap guns	100-300	700
Alarm guns	50-125	300
Small advertising items	10-75	150

All items should be pre-1950, original, 80% or better condition and complete. The older the better. I do not want reproductions, badly damaged items, "How to Trap" publications and price lists.

Prices Paid by: Ron Willoughby
1072 Route 171
Woodstock, CT 06281   (203) 974-1226
I will answer all letters and calls. I am fair, honest and a very serious collector. I am in a position to purchase single items or entire estates.

Ammunition & Bombs

Ammunition collecting is a small part of the much larger gun collecting hobby. There are about 5,000 formal collectors worldwide and hundreds of thousands of closet collectors who have a small collection to augment their gun hobby. Most ammunition is not very valuable but there are hundreds of types which are. I collect all types of ammunition from small arms through heavy artillery, grenades, mines, bombs and the fuses which ignite them. I also collect all forms of reference material in all languages for the subject; books, manuals, photos, films and tapes are all of value to me. The following price ranges depend upon three things: 1) what the item is, 2) the condition of the item, 3) loading.

SMALL ARMS AMMUNITION

This is the most popular field of collecting and includes items from .10 caliber through 36 mm in projectile diameter.

One inch Gatling	$50-1,000
One inch Nordenfeldt	50-200
.69 Crittenden and Tibbals	2000
Boxes of Crittenden and Tibbals ammo	200-5000
11 mm Japanese Murata	100-350
8 mm Japanese Murata	200-450
25 mm Russian AA gun	110-250
20 mm U.S. Marquart aircraft cannon	100-350
20 mm experimental combustible case	100-350
30 mm combustible case	100-350
Soviet 7.62 mm silenced cartridge	500
Soviet 5.45 underwater flechette	250
Flechette (small arrow) projectile-type cartridges	25-250

ARTILLERY AMMUNITION

This kind of ammunition collecting, projectiles range up to 2500 pounds and diameters to 18 inches.

18 inch Japanese battleship	$1,000
18 inch U.S. experimental	1,000
16 inch U.S.	150-1,000
16 inch U.S. brass case	5,000
80 cm German railway gun projectile	5,000
Case	5,000
Experimental rounds	1,000-5,000
120 mm tank	100-500
Soviet 125 mm tank	350-750
140 mm tank	350-750
Atomic projectiles	250-2,500
60 mm Israel Merkava tank	100-350
German 88 mm tank, antitank, anti aircraft types	200-750

GRENADES

(loaded grenades are worthless to me and could send you to jail or the cemetery.) Inert (unloaded) only!

U.S. pre WWI	$200-500
U.S. WWI MK 1 type frag	50-100
U.S. WWI gas	50-100
U.S. WWI rifle types	100-250
German WWI potato masher	100-250
German WWII potato masher	100-250
Japanese pre WWII types	100-500
Japanese WWII types	25-150
Soviet pre WWII types	100-350
Soviet WWII types	35-200
Soviet post WWII and current	50-350
Viet Nam War (Viet Cong, Chinese, Cambodian, Thai)	50-250

GRENADE LAUNCHER

Large projectiles fired from a fixed case like small arms ammo. U.S. M 79 is the most common.

M 79 high explosive	$35-100
M 79 (40 mm) antenna cartridge	25-100
M 79 (40 mm) rocket cartridge	100-250
M 79 (40 mm) experimental types	50-350

ROCKETS

Ground, sea and aircraft types.

WWII German R4M	$500
Soviet SA 7	500
U.S. Redeye	500
U.S. Stinger	500
Soviet, Chinese and their allies RPG 2	250-750
RPG 7	250
Later and current TYPES	
RPG 16, 18, 24, etc.	200-2,000
Experimental types	100-5,000

SUBMUNITIONS

Small bomblets or minelets which are delivered by artillery shell

Rocket or bomb	$25-500

AIRCRAFT BOMBS $50-5000

FUSES

Artillery types	$25-200
Bomb	25-200
Soviet proximity types	200-500
Experimental	50-1,000

NAVAL MINES & FUSES $100-5,000

It is best to send a rough drawing and description of size and markings. A detail sheet is available upon request which will help to describe any item of ammunition.

I collect all types, countries and eras from the stone cannon ball to current guided projectiles and have been a major collector of this material for over 35 years.

Dr. Crittenden Schmitt is the contributing editor for Artillery and Explosive Ordnance for the International Ammunition Journal, official publication of the International Ammunition Association, Inc. and Director of Crittenden Schmitt Archives as well as a technical consultant to the Smithsonian Institution and other museums, industry, government and entertainment organizations.

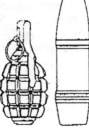

Prices Paid by: Dr. Crittenden Schmitt
Courthouse Post Office Box 4253
Rockville, MD 20850

Bossons Figures

Bossons wall sculptures, faces, or heads are highly coveted, strong plaster, hand painted figurines. Collectors want discontinued models. They are often found with nicks, or have been severely damaged by amateur painting. Except in rare cases, the earliest Bossons were incised with 1958 or 1959 "Bossons Copyright Reserved, Congleton, England," and those produced after 1960 have names incised below the neckline on the collar. Suggested retail prices sampled below are based on three important considerations: (1) our cost; (2) our known rarity; and (3) the time it has taken Don to restore Bossons to original beauty @ $40 per hour:

Series A:

Snake Charmer, 1958-59, 10"	from $150-750
Bengali, c. 1970, 10 1/2",	
very rare	3,500-5,200
Mandolin player, 1959, 10"	
(light or dark)	175-300
Abduhl, 1961, 8"	
(any version hat stripes)	75-125

Series B:

Caspian man, 1959, 7"	$125-200
Corsican, C. 1959, 5 1/2"	85-150
Syrian, 1960 (1st model,	
still in production)	27-32
Romany, 1st ed., 1960, 8 1/2"	150-185
2nd ed., 1969, 11 1/2"	
(retired 1992)	130
Cavalier (red or green feather),	
c. 1959, 8"	300-500
Gibbon (Wildlife series), 1967, 11"	250-350

Bengali "King of Bossons"
$3,500 - $5,200

WANTED TO BUY — RARE BOSSONS

Don pays from $100-3000. Call for information:

Bossons pottery products: Disney Characters– Mickey, Donald Duck, Garden, Figure, Pooch Dog, Jazz Figures, Miniature African figures. Various clocks and mirrors. Desert Hawks (original coloring). Geisha and Madonna Plaques. French Poodle, black. Setter, Scottie and Mac Dogs. Afghan, Yussef and Sophie, 8", shelf ornaments. Sophie and other lamp bases. Churchill. Series B, 5 1/2", gilded. Beefeater, 1966. Original Lemurs. Berber 12" shelf ornament. Fraser-Art: Swan; Linebacker and Bronco; Horses; Richard Neville; and Saluki. SMALL Briar Rose Animals, Large Hippo, & Giraffe; early scenic plaques.

Bare Arm Cheyenne Indian

Paul Kruger

Value in Bossons collectibles is the same as with all coveted, retired antiques and is determined by demand, condition, and how much the collector will pay, and the seller will accept. Records indicate that "only about 50 Bengali were made." Documented RETAIL sales for PERFECT CONDITION Bengali from Don's Collectibles over a seven-year period follows: LOW-Jan. 1986 = $2800; HIGH-Apr. 1990 = $5200; and MEDIAN-June, 1993 = $3600; AVERAGE sales value of Bengali = $3827.

Usually made of plaster, retired Bossons often require restorations. Dr. Don Hardisty, Professor of Music, Emeritus, New Mexico State University, has collected and studied Bossons for over 25 years. As an internationally recognized authority on Bossons, he is recommended by Bossons to restore their products. While referencing mint and perfect condition Bossons, Don applies his artistic abilities using modern scientific equipment and with meticulous and artistically sensitive strokes makes these fantastic characters come to life.

Avid, investment-minded collectors build their entire collections with Don's assistance because they trust him for excellent condition, authentic products at market-tested prices.

Beauty is hard to define – but you'll know it when you see Bossons from Don.

Prices Paid by:	Don Hardisty	
	3020 Majestic Ridge	1-800-BOSSONS
	Las Cruces, NM 88011	FAX (505) 522-7909

Tokens and Medals, Etc.

Saloon Trade Token

Indian Peace Medal

Slave Tag

If YOU are interested in getting the best price for your tokens, medals, badges, ribbons, pin-back buttons, advertising mirrors, World's Fair collectibles, Franklin Mint issues and other similar small collectibles, I am BUYING all types and quantities. I collect many areas, and have thousands of collectors wanting to buy your material. We also accept better material for auction. A sample copy of our recent mail bid sale catalog (color cover, almost $200,000 in sales) is available for only $9 postpaid, and includes the prices realized. We prefer items worth about $15 each and up for auction. If you are interested in consignment, please send a brief description of your material and a S.A.S.E. for full information. Collectors: Please write!

SELLING: Please SHIP for my top offer of your material. As condition does make a significant difference on price on many items, we really do prefer to see your material prior to making a firm offer. If you absolutely must have an estimate prior to shipment, send an S.A.S.E. and clear photocopies and/or descriptions for my general estimate. Due to the number of inquiries, I am unable to devote much time to price solicitations, and regret it is impossible to offer the best price from your photocopy or listing. I really do want to buy ALL of your material, and encourage you to ship for my top offer. Prices listed here are generally for the most common item and should be considered minimums.

COMMON MATERIAL

While I will buy all quantities, many items are extremely common to me, and are often thought to be worth substantially more by the uninformed. Some rarities do exist in some of these categories, and I am most interested in scarce to rare items. Prices shown are for nice, undamaged condition, delivered. Write on large quantities. I SELL all of these items at modest prices, in quantities of 100 or more (send S.A.S.E. for price list):

Type	Number Made	Price Paid for Common
Sales Tax Tokens	Several BILLION	3¢
OPA red/blue tokens	3 BILLION	1¢
Transportation	Usually 100,000 up	5¢ (up to 10 of each)
Video arcade	Millions made	1¢
Wooden nickels	Usually 1000 of each	5¢
Shell "Presidents"	Millions made	3¢

Common transportation tokens are the dime and quarter sized pieces, often with cut-outs. A very few of this type are worth more. I SELL 100 different, all metal transit tokens for $19.95, and 2500 mixed for $99.95 postpaid (in stock, just send a check). RARE transit tokens have horse-cars, or state "Good for Round Trip," or "Hotel-Depot," or similar and are worth $10 up to $1500 each. Please Ship!

SCARCE TO RARE MATERIAL

I am much more interested in buying scarce to rare items, and will pay my best price for such items. Due to the huge numbers of items issued, I can only list minimum prices for each category. Some sample prices paid for better items are also listed. I am the top buyer for all better tokens, medals, etc. To get the best price for your items, ship today!

• **Trade Tokens** ("Good For" something): Paying 35¢ each and up for common pieces in small quantities, for those with a city and state. Large quantities wanted (send sample and quantity). I will pay $1 to $10 and up for each metal trade token needed (small towns, mostly), more for smaller and western states. I am BUYING all U.S. and world tokens at highly competitive prices. Collections and hoards are wanted.

• **Saloon Tokens** (MUST have the word "Saloon" on the token). I will pay at least $13 each for virtually all early Saloon tokens, more for Western states, more for pieces with pictorials, etc. I will pay $75 for a Rockford IL area Saloon, and will pay $30 up for any Illinois or Wisconsin Saloon token I need ($20 for most duplicates). Paying $50 up for "A.T." or "I.T." tokens. Also buying Bar, Tavern, Coal, Lumber and other tokens. Ship!

• **Hard Times–Civil War Tokens:** Will pay $3.50 to $10 up for common pieces.

• **Dog Tags:** I will pay $25 up for pre-1901 tags; $3.50-$10 up for 1901-09; $2.50 up for 1910-19; $1.50 up for 1920-29; 75¢-$1 up for 1930-39; 35¢-50¢ for 1940-59, and 15¢-25¢ for 1960 up. Large quantities wanted (write). Seeking cat, rabies (1¢ each), other animal tags. Higher prices paid for Rockford area tags needed. Ship!

• **Civil War Dog Tags:** Paying $200 up for awarded; $500 up for named corps badges.

• **Other:** Also seeking encased coins, elongated coins, celluloid advertising, bicycle advertising & medals, Bryan Money, Inaugural Medals, Military Medals, watch fobs.

• **Credit Cards:** I've collected for almost 20 years, and seriously want to buy! Paying 50¢-$1 each for recent/current plastics, $2.50-$5.00 for Charge-plates, $4-$15 for metal charge tokens, up to $150 each for celluloid. Ship any quantity.

• **Advertising Mirrors:** All types of pocket and paperweight celluloid advertising mirrors are wanted! Paying $45-$100 up for most "Good For" mirrors. Mirrors with females, products depicted, or scenes are especially wanted, most at $10-$50 up. Plain mirrors with wording only are worth $10-$25 each. Most rectangular mirrors are $1-$5 each.

• **Awarded Medals:** Any and all U.S. or world medals with hand engraving are wanted at serious prices. All gold and silver medals are wanted, especially before 1901. All other medals are also wanted. Olympic medals and souvenirs especially wanted (pre-1960). Will pay $2,500 for the 1904 Olympic medal, $3,000 if awarded with box.

• **Indian Peace Medals:** I will pay $1,250-$10,000 for genuine silver I.P. medals. Also seeking original copper medals, and all U.S. Mint issues. I wrote the PRICE GUIDE!

• **World's Fair Material:** As there are so many items, it is virtually impossible to list prices paid. I am most interested in pre-1940 items, but NOT in most paper: books, pamphlets or postcards (except large collections). I seek badges, pinbacks, tokens, medals, playing cards, ribbons, tickets, china, watches, letterheads, fobs, bottles, fans and all larger items, especially the unusual, awarded and engraved items, or in silver or gold.

- **Badges & Ribbons:** I am MOST interested in all singles and quantities of all types of plain to fancy badges and ribbons from World's Fairs ($10-100 up), G.A.R. ($2-10 up), Masonic (50¢-$5 up), Confederate ($10 up), 8-hour day ($15 up), Mining related, Labor related and all other fraternal items such as banners (no uniforms or swords).

- **Chauffeur Badges:** Will pay $45 up for most early undated badges; $20 up for most pre-1920 badges; $2 each for Minnesota; $5 up for other sates, with original pins.

- **Franklin Mint Issues:** I am seriously interested in buying all modern mint issues, including medals, bars, plates, figurines, etc., at current prices. Ship any quantity.

- **Political Material:** Since condition is highly critical on pinbacks, I MUST see them prior to making any offer. Buying all types of political tokens, medals, pinbacks, china, ribbons, canes, badges, silks, etc. Please ship for my top offer. Sorry, no offers from lists.

- **Masonic & Fraternal:** All Masonic pennies, medals, badges, miniature trowels ($5-8) wanted. Paying $200 for gold pennies, $5 for silver, $2-5 up for others. Paying $50-150 for early hand engraved silver badges. Buying all fobs, pins, spoons and early china. All fraternal items wanted, esp. Knights of Labor ($40 up!). Please ship!

- **Slave Tags:** Call COLLECT immediately! I am the highest buyer!

- **DUN (and Bradstreet) Oversized Commercial Directories:** Paying $100 up for pre-1901 all-state directories; $50 for 1901-20; $50 for 1921-30. Pre-1960 wanted! Ship!

- **Rockford, Freeport, Belvidere Items Wanted!** Will pay $2500 for a mint Baier and Ohlendorf tin sign. All signs, tins, tokens, medals, badges, ribbons, etc wanted!

- **Counterstamped Coins:** With names stamped on coins: Paying $5-5000 each.

- **Mining Related:** I am seriously interested in buying ribbons, badges and other items from Mining organizations: UMWofA; UMMWUofNA; WFofM; Miners Union; United Mineworkers; Eight-Hour Day, etc. Will pay $30 up for each ribbon/badge. Also buying tokens and medals, esp. early and awarded/engraved pieces. Pressed coal items wanted. Buying miner's lamps and oil wicks, etc.

BUYING GUIDE

I offer a **FREE** Buying Guide, with minimum prices paid by category, with details of specific items I am seeking. Send $3 for immediate shipment, or send two stamps for a free copy when published. For the ultimate in pricing information on tokens and medals, buy the book **Identification and Values of US Tokens and Medals**, with prices for hundreds of categories, 320 pages, illustrated. Only $22.50 postpaid. I also stock most books on tokens and medals, if you are interested in learning more, or collecting. Send two stamps for a current list.

I want to BUY your material. I want to buy everything in the above categories, and will do my best to make you a top offer. In 1993 I purchased 99.6% of all material sent to me. I have been seriously buying since 1975, and have purchased over three million items! Don't spend the time making a list, just box it all up and ship today with your price desired, or for my very best offer. I will travel to purchase significant collections. Thank You!

Prices Paid by:	Rich Hartzog	
	World Exonumia	
	POB 4143BPH	
	Rockford, IL 61110-0643	(815) 226-0771
		FAX: (815) 397-7662

Stock Certificates and Bonds

The collecting of defunct and worthless stocks and bonds is a relatively small collecting field compared to coins or stamps. Still, there are people who enjoy collecting these colorful relics of Wall Street's yesterdays.

A number of things determine the collector value of old securities. These are 1) age; 2) attractiveness; 3) type of industry represented (mining, railroad, etc); 4) condition; 5) region or state the certificate is from.

America West Archives is buying old Stock Certificates and Bonds
Mining - Railroad - Automotive - Energy and other industries are wanted

---

Listed below is an example of the prices we will pay for issued, pre-1930 stocks and bonds:

Issued stocks dated 1915-1930 - will pay $2-5 each

Issued stocks dated 1900-1915 - will pay $5-15 each

Issued stocks dated 1880-1899 - will pay $10-30 each

Issued stocks dated 1850-1879 - will pay $15-40 each

We are buying American stocks and bonds only.
We are not interested in certificates from Canada or any other country.

SELLING YOUR OLD STOCKS AND BONDS ARE AS EASY AS
ONE, TWO, THREE!

First, make photocopies of your certificates (front only). If you have numerous pieces from the same company, just make a copy of one & tell us how many total pieces you have. Then mail the photocopies to us - be sure to include your phone number. When we receive the copies, we will call you and make an offer. You can then either accept or decline the offer. It's that simple!

We are also buying other old financial paper and documents including bank checks, bank drafts, certificates of deposit also documents, letters, maps, photographs and many other types of old papers.

Prices Paid by: Warren Anderson
American West Archives
PO Box 100   Days (801) 586-9497
Cedar City, Utah 84721   Nights (801) 586-7323

Books & Catalogs

TRADE CATALOGS show goods and materials for sale. I try not to buy those issued after 1920. Standard Bibliographic format required.

Khomiakoff, Moskovka, Stem Engine, London, 1851	50
Amer. Road Machine. Illus. Cat., 1891, 32pp. 5x8"	25
•Fairbanks-Morse Home Water Service, 1934, 32pp. 10x8"	8
Albany Cotton Gin Circular, 1868, 24pps., 10x8", edge nawed	20

TUNE BOOKS WITH SHAPED NOTES If unfamiliar, don't worry; see illustration. My interest is only for those printed prior to 1900, 5 or 6" high and 9" across. Don't be discouraged by the dates; I do buy later editions, proportionately priced.

Boyd, J.S., *Virginia Sacred Musical*, 1816	$200
Carrell, *J.P., Songs of Zion*, 18120	200
Clayton/Carrell, *Virginia Harmony*, 1831	150
Davisson, *Kentucky Harmony*, 1816	150
Please request an author and title list.	

SHEET MUSIC... BOUND VOLUMES ONLY These are usually 19th century and the price paid depends on the number and quality of items bound in. Important to note any staining, tears, or repairs to pages. Helpful to note any illust. covers (note if hand tinted). When describing, brief titles are fine.

Telegraph Waltzes, c. 1847, 7p.	$12
Old Rough and Ready Quick Step, 1846, 2p.	8
•Welcome Home, 1848, 4p.	5
Perabeau, Honour to the Brave, 1846	15

SPANISH AMERICAN WAR All types of memorabilia, including proceedings of Sp/Am War Vets. Association. CAUTION: Buying for one customer, and you must allow time for me to write to and hear from; then I can respond to you. This customer does not buy newspapers. Below are items already bought for him.

Armstrong, *Pictorial Atlas Sp/Am War*, 1898	$50
•White, *Our War With Spain*	5
Santiago Campaign, 1927	16
Sp/Am War by US War Dept, 1899	13
•*Ditto. Vets. Ritual*, 1928	4

CIVIL WAR AND 1ST PERSON NARRATIVES Condition is important.

Davis, *Rise and Fall/Confed. Govt.*, 2 vols.	$75
•Johnston, *Life/Albert Sidney johnston*	35
Jackson, *Life/Letters...Stonewall*, 1892	75
Lee, *Memoirs Wm. Nelson Pendleton*, 1893	50

SOUTHERN IMPRINTS/TITLES Pre-1860. Please use Standard Bibliographic form. These can be books printed in the south or about.

Thomas, J., *White Pilgrim*, Winchester, VA, 1813	$100
Howison, *Hist. of Virginia*, 2 vols.	100
So. Lit. Messenger (Magazine) per volume	20-100

APPALACHIAN AUTHORS Customers believe dust jackets are so important, even though they constitute less than one percent of most books. But tell me about your book, even if no jacket.

Post, M.D., Strange Schemes	$25
Miles, Emma, Spirit of the Mountains	50
Simpson, Mountain Path	50

NEALE BOOKS (PUBLISHER) Most have that name printed at the bottom of backstrip. CAUTION: many of the Neal bindings were vary attractive to insects, and the best way to describe is to photocopy the covers and on the print darken in the flecked areas. Neale published nearly 100 Civil War titles and nearly 30 on Virginia.

Anderson, *Fighting by So. Federals*	$35
Ford, *Life in the Confederate Army*	50
O'Ferral, *Forty Years of Active Service*	25
Polley, *Soldier's Letters to Charming Nellie*	200

TECHNICAL BOOKS BEFORE 1920 Many of my customers have a real love affair going with 19th or early 20th century grain mills, house building, weaving, optical instrumentation, carriages, coffins, or cabooses. Most of these books were single topic (not a dictionary or general book); a book on the telegraph is of more interest than one on communication.

Watson, *British... Building Btones*, 1911	$18
Ruhmkoff Induction Coils, 1896	75
Henry, *Elements of Exper. Chem.*, 1817	60
•Monteath, *new... System of Draining*, 1829	35
Holtzapffel, *Turning and Mech. Manip.*, 6 vols. 1852+	250

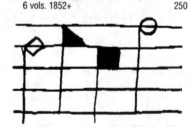

Notes are triangle, diamond, square & round.

Prices Paid by: Jim Presgraves, ABAA
Bookworm & Silverfish
P.O. Box 639
Wytheville, VA 24382

If you want to know more about me, there's a business/bio I can send. I appreciate your interest.

Children's Books

Series books come in two basic formats. Most series books copyright before 1960 should have a paper cover, called a dust jacket. Books printed after 1960 may come in a style called "pictorial cover." These books have a drawing in color on the front cover. The prices listed are for books in fine (as new) condition in like dust jackets. Pictorial cover books are noted p/c.

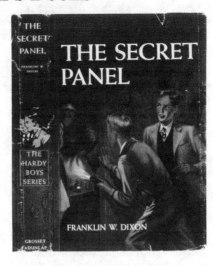

Nancy Drew	#s	1-40	$3-10
depending on age and style of dust jacket			
Nancy Drew	p/c		1-1.50
Judy Bolton	p/c #s	30-38	5-20
Hardy Boys	#s	1-41	3-10
with fine D.J.			
Bobbsey Twins	#s	1-54	2-3
Bobbsey Twins	p/c		1
Chip Hilton	#s	1-19	3-10
Chip Hilton	#s	20-23	
p/c			10-50
Tom Swift, Sr.	#s	1-40	3-10
Tom Swift, Jr.	#s	30-33	
p/c			10-20
Rick Brant	#s	20-24	
p/c			10-50
Rick Brant	#s	4-19	2-8

For most series with dust jackets, we will pay a minimum of $2 & postage. Please contact us for price quote. SASE appreciated.

If you have a more valuable book, we will tell you and pay accordingly.

Encyclopedias

Encyclopedia Judaica, 1972	$125
Inquire for other years	
Encyclopedia Britannica, 1993	250
1992	200
Great books	
depending on binding	75-100

We do not purchase The Book of Knowledge, Comptons, Colliers, supermarket sets, Household, Mother's, etc.

Heritage Press

Must be fine (as new) condition, in original fine box, with Sandglass letter laid in. We buy most titles in lots as they are worth only $2-3 each. Some special ones are:

Gone With The Wind, 2 vol.	$12
Lewis and Clark, 2 vol.	12
Book of Ruth, Job	6 each

Limited Editions Club

Must be in fine (as new) condition, in original fine box.

Lysistrata	$400
Ulysses	400
Wind In The Willows	150
Voice of the City	100
Shakespeare 37 vols.	250
Through the Looking Glass	150

Please call or write about other titles. There are over 500 titles.

We buy books in all fields except medicine and law. If you send SASE, we will help you sell your books, even if we can't use them, provided they have intrinsic value.

Prices Paid by: Lee Temares
50 Heights Road
Plandome, NY 11030
Call to alert us to turn fax on.

8 AM-12 Midnight EST (516) 627-8688
FAX: (516) 627-7822

Price Guides to Collectibles

Readers tell us they would like to know more about what they are selling, and they'd feel more comfortable if they had some idea of an item's worth before offering it for sale. We were asked for help.

So we contacted authors, publishers and wholesalers and made arrangements to make some popular collectibles books available to you. Now you too can use the books used by antique dealers thanks to hassle free shopping.

It's easy to order. Select the information you want and fill out the order form. We find the book for you, order it, and it arrives on your doorstep. It's that easy.

IMPORTANT: **we do not stock books offered in this guidebook.** When we receive your order, we promptly order your book from the publisher via fax. It is quickly shipped to you by the author or publisher within a few days. Since every book you order is a special order for us, we cannot accept returns of books. We always order the newest and latest edition for you. Books damaged in shipment will be replaced by the shipper with another copy of the same title.

All customers must add $4 per book to cover postage and handling. This helps cover our costs for the valuable service of listing price guides that are available, locating books, ordering them, and having them shipped to you. Send a check, money order or your MC/VISA number and expiration date. Orders are handled promptly.

MC/VISA **customers** may order by phone Monday through Friday by calling (805) 773-6777 from 9am to 5pm Pacific. You may also order by fax at (805) 773-8436. If you prefer to use mail, make sure you don't forget the expiration date on the card. We are a family-run company and handle your card information with care. All banking is electronic so there is no paper trail or carbon copies to worry about.

California customers add sales tax of 8 1/4% (83¢ per $10).

Canadian customers, because your higher postal rates (and the high number of packages lost in transit), we must charge an additional $3 per book. When you can, it is a lot easier for us if you pay with a Postal Money Order in U.S. dollars. You may also use a check drawn on a U.S. bank in U.S. funds. If you must pay by check in Canadian dollars, add 30% to the price of the book to cover exchange rate loss and foreign banking fees. All prices are in U.S. dollars.

Twentieth Century Fashionable
PLASTIC JEWELRY
Lillian Baker
ISBN: 0-89145-493-4
Virtually every aspect of collecting this prized plastic jewelry is covered in great detail. Color photos, glossary of terms and types, current values and original company material fill this complex guide. 1992 values.
#2348 • 8½ x 11 • 240 Pgs. • HB • $19.95

ADVERTISING CHARACTER COLLECTIBLES
An Identification and Value Guide
Warren Dotz
ISBN: 0-89145-531-0
More than 400 memorable trademark advertising characters presented in beautiful full color. As a celebration of advertising design, this guide provides an entertaining and invaluable reference source for collectors. 1993 values.
#3427 • 8½ x 11 • 160 Pgs. • PB • $17.95

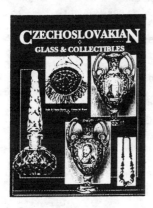

CZECHOSLOVAKIAN
Glass & Collectibles
Dale & Diane Barta and Helen M. Rose
ISBN: 0-89145-483-7
This guide not only includes this beautiful glass but also purses, jewelry, pottery, porcelain, china, lamps, and other collectibles featured in full color. Complete histories, descriptions, dates, and values. 1992 values.
#2275 • 8½ x11 • 152 Pgs. • PB • $16.95

Guide to
COOKBOOK COLLECTING
Colonel Bob Allen
ISBN: 0-89145-421-7
A well researched guide for cookbook collectors, loaded with histories, dates, sizes, and current values. Hundreds of examples are photographed in full color. 1993 values.
#2081 • 8½ x 11 • 216 Pgs. • PB • $14.95

PRICE GUIDES ON COLLECTIBLES

GENERAL PRICE GUIDE

3737 **Schroeder's Antiques Price Guide** -Latest Edition-New   12.95
sources-Over 50,000 listings with current values in over 500
categories-81/2x11-608 Pgs.

FURNITURE, RUGS & LAMPS

2132 **Collector's Ency. of American Furniture, Vol. I, -The**   24.95
Darkwoods -Swedberg-Includes full color examples of cherry,
mahogany, rosewood & walnut-1993 current values-81/2x11-128
Pgs.-(HB)

2271 **Collector's Encyclopedia of American Furniture, Vol.**   24.95
II -Furniture of the 20th Century-Swedberg-450 color photos
descriptions, sizes, dates & 1992 values-144 Pgs.-81/2x11-(HB)

1755 **Furniture of the Depression Era** -Swedberg-350+ photos of   19.95
20's, 30's & 40's-1994 values-(HB)

2394 **Oil Lamps II, Glass Kerosene Lamps** -800 lamps in full color   24.95
with 1992 separate Price Guide-(HB)

1965 **Pine Furniture, Our American Heritage** -McNerney-100's of   14.95
photos-Current values-81/2x11-176 Pgs.

1885 **Victorian Furniture, Our American Heritage** -McNerney-   9.95
1994 current values-51/2x81/2-256 Pgs.

1457 **American Oak Furniture** -McNerney-Over 400 photos-   9.95
Descriptions, sizes & dates for all photographs-Also included
1994 values-51/2x81/2-176 Pgs.-(HB)

KITCHEN & HOUSEHOLD ITEMS

1782 **1,000 Fruit Jars, 5th Ed.** -Schroeder-1994 values-Brought   5.95
back by popular demand-51/2x81/2

3359 **300 Years of Housekeeping Collectibles** -3rd Ed.-Franklin-   22.95
Fully illustrated-81/2x11-216 Pgs.

2299 **300 Years of Kitchen Collectibles** -3rd Ed.-Franklin-Doubled   22.95
in size-Completely revised-81/2x11-640 Pgs.

1712 **Antique & Collectible Thimbles & Accessories** -Mathis-   19.95
700+ Items in full color-81/2x11-176 Pgs.-(HB)

2269 **Antique Brass & Copper Collectibles** -Gaston-Over 500 full   16.95
color photos-2 books in 1-81/2x11-208 Pgs.

1880 **Antique Iron** -McNerney-Cast iron collectibles-Over 400   9.95
photos-1993 values-224 Pgs.

3717 **Christmas Collectible** -Whitmyer-Over 1,000 full color photos   24.95
containing virtually every type Christmas collectible 1,000's of
current values-81/2x11-304 Pgs.-(HB)

1752 **Christmas Ornaments, Lights & Decorations** -Johnson-Over   19.95
750 full color photos including 1,000's of items- Chapters on
storage, repairing, telling old from new, histories, types & much
more-81/2x11-318 Pgs.-(HB)

2018 **Collector's Ency. of Granite Ware** -Greguire-Over 180 full   24.95
color photos containing everything from bread boxes to teapots-
Dates, sizes, histories & 1992 values-81/2x11-414 Pgs.-(HB)

1373 **Collector's Encyclopedia of American Dinnerware** -   24.95
Cunningham-100's of pieces photographed in full color & black
& white-Complete histories-1992 values-81/2x11-322 Pgs.-(HB)

PRICE GUIDES ON COLLECTIBLES

| |

2133 **Collector's Encyclopedia of Cookie Jars** -Roerig-Over 1,000   24.95
full color examples-Large text-Descriptions- 100's of manufactur-
ers included-1993 values-81/2x11-312 Pgs.-(HB)

1629 **Doorstops, Id & Values** -Bertoia-300+ Full color photos-176   9.95
Pgs.-1993 values

2081 **Guide to Collecting Cookbooks** -Allen-full color examples-   14.95
Histories, dates & 1993 values-176 Pgs.

2340 **Guide to Easter Coll.** -Burnett-100's of F/C examples from   16.95
1800's to present-Current values-124 Pgs.

2216 **Kitchen Antiques, 1790-1940** -McNerney-650 excellent pho-   14.95
tos containing virtually every kitchen item since the 1790's-
Complete descriptions, sizes, dates, histories-1994 values-
81/2x11-224 Pgs.

2041 **Old Lace & Linens, Id. & Value Guide** -Dolan-Fully   10.95
illustrated-51/2x81/2-156 Pgs.

2080 **Price Guide to Cookbooks & Recipe Leaflets** -Dickinson-   9.95
Photos-1993 values-192 Pgs.

2096 **Silverplated Flatware** -Revised 4th Ed.-Hagan-Over 1,500   14.95
illustrations of different patterns-For each illustration included are
values for the fork,knife & spoon-Manufacturer dated & marks
are included-81/2x11-372 Pgs.

1875 **Sterling Silver, Silverplate and Souvenir Spoons** -Old   12.95
catalog reprints-187 Pgs.

2224 **World of Salt Shakers** -2nd Ed.-Lechner-250+ f/color photos-   24.95
Descriptions & facts-81/2x11-312 Pgs.-(HB)

WATCHES, JEWELRY & ACCESSORIES

3806 **Collecting Rhinestone Jewelry Id. & Value Guide** -3rd Ed.-   22.95
Dolan-Completely revised-81/2x11-330 Pgs.

1797 **Comic Character Clocks & Watches** -Brenner-122 Pgs.   14.95

3831 **Complete Guide to Watches** -14th Ed.-Shugart-35,000   19.95
values-7,400 illus.51/2x81/2-1064 Pgs.

1716 **Fifty Years of Collectible Fashion Jewelry, 1925-1975** -   19.95
Baker-Photos of 25 different collections-Current values-191
Pgs.(HB)

1424 **Hatpins & Hatpin Holders** -Baker-Full color-160 Pgs.-1994   9.95
values

2348 **20th Century Fashionable Plastic Jewelry** -Baker-1,000's of   19.95
current values-81/2x11-240 Pgs.-(HB)

GLASSWARE

2016 **Bedroom & Bathroom Glassware of the Depression Yrs.**   19.95
-Whitmyer-300+ full color photos-1,000's of items included-
1992 values-One of our better selling glass titles-81/2x11-254
Pgs.(HB)

2310 **Children's Glass Dishes, China & Furniture, Vol. I** -   19.95
Lechler-1993 values-100's of photos-81/2x11-(HB)

1627 **Children's Glass Dishes, China & Furniture, Vol. II** -   19.95
Lechler-1,000's items photo'd-1993 values-(HB)

3719 **Coll. Glassware from the 40's, 50's & 60's** -Florence-2nd   19.95
Ed.-100's of new items photographed-32 additional pgs.-58
different patterns-81/2x11-192 Pgs.-(HB)

PRICE GUIDES ON COLLECTIBLES

Cat#		Price
3724	**Collector's Ency. of Depression Glass** -1992 11th Ed.- Florence-4,000+ pieces w/current values & f/color photos & finds-81/2x11-224 Pgs.-# 1 bestselling glass books-(HB)-	19.95
1810	**Collector's Encyclopedia of American Art Glass** -Shuman- 700+ full color photos-Marks section- 1994 values-81/2x11-336 Pgs.-(HB)	29.95
1843	**Covered Animal Dishes** -Grist-200 full color photos-1993 values-81/2x11-120 Pgs.	14.95
2275	**Czechoslovakian Glass & Coll.** -Barta-Full color-Current values-includes purses, lamps, china, jewelry & more	16.95
3318	**Glass Animals of the Depression Era** -Including Figural Flower Frogs & Reissues-Garmon & Spencer-1,000's of examples in full color-Current values-81/2x11-240 Pgs.-(HB)–Will become THE book on this subject1	19.95
2024	**Kitchen Glassware of the Depression Years** -4th Edition, Florence-Full color- Over 3,000 pieces of glass listing size, color, pattern description-Current values-(HB)-	19.95
3322	**Pocket Guide to Depression Glass** 8th Ed.-Florence-Over 4,000 values-100's of full color photos- Considered much more than a pocket guide-51/2x81/2-160 Pgs.	9.95
3739	**Standard Carnival Glass Encyclopedia** -Revised 4th Ed.- Edwards-Over 1,000 pieces photographed in full color- Contains all Carnival Glass manufacturers-current values-81/2x11-288 Pgs.-(HB)	24.95

POTTERY

Cat#		Price
1358	**Collector's Ency. of McCoy Pottery** -Huxford-Over 1,200 pieces of McCoy photographed in full color-Complete marks-1993 values-81/2x11-247 Pgs.-(HB)	19.95
1312	**Blue and White Stoneware-McNerney** -152 Pgs.-1993 values-51/2x81/2	9.95
1311	**Coll. Ency of R.S. Prussia, 1st Series** -Gaston-Full color photos-1993 values-81/2x11-216 Pgs.-(HB)	24.95
2272	**Coll. Ency. of California Pottery** -Chipman-300 color photos of 1,000's of pieces- Marks section-81/2x11-160 Pgs.-(HB)	24.95
3837	**Coll. Ency. of Nippon Porcelain I** -Joan Van Patten-81/2 x 11-222 Pgs.-F/color-1994 values-(HB)	24.95
1447	**Coll. Ency. of Noritake** -Van Patten-450+ color photos-Mark Section-1994 values-200 Pgs.-(HB)	19.95
1037	**Coll. Ency. of Occupied Japan, Vol. I** -Florence-Full color-1992 values-81/2x11-108 Pgs.-(PB)	14.95
2111	**Coll. Ency. of Weller Pottery** -Huxford-1,000+ pieces illus. in f/color-1994 value guide-81/2x11-375 Pgs.-(HB)	29.95
2339	**Coll. Guide To Shawnee Pottery** -Vanderbilt-Over 400 color photos-1994 values- Complete histories-81/2x11-144 Pgs.-(HB)	19.95
2209	**Collector's Ency. of Fiesta** -1994 Ed.-Huxford-Full color-Expanded to 81/2x11 hardbound-Many new photos-Most complete book ever produced on this subject-190 Pgs.-(HB)	19.95
1276	**Collector's Ency. of Hull Pottery** -Roberts-Over 2,500 items photographed in full color-Descriptions for 116 Hull lines with dates & complete histories are included-1993 values-81/2x11-207 Pgs.-(HB)	19.95

PRICE GUIDES ON COLLECTIBLES

Cat#

1959   **Blue Willow** -Revised 2nd Ed.-Gaston-400+ f/color photos-   14.95
1992 values-81/2x11-169 Pgs.

1034   **Collector's Ency. of Roseville Pottery** -Huxford-Over 2,500   19.95
full color items-1993 values bound in back-Completely illustrated
Marks Section-One of our most popular pottery books-81/2x11-
192 Pgs.-(HB)

1035   **Collector's Ency. of Roseville Pottery, Vol. 2** -Huxford-No   19.95
repeats of above-Over 2,500 items photographed in full with 1993
values-Complete marks section-81/2x11-207 Pgs.-(HB)

1917   **Head Vases, Id. & Values** -Cole-Over 800 full color examples-   14.95
1994 values-81/2x11-142 Pgs.

DOLLS

2300   **Antique Collector's Dolls, Vol. I** -Smith-1991 values-   17.95
81/2x11-320 Pgs.

2301   **Antique Collector's Dolls, Vol. II** -Smith-1991 values-   17.95
81/2x11-272 Pgs.

2079   **Barbie Doll Fashions, Vol. I** -Eames-100's clothes pho-   24.95
tographed in full color with current values-Complete histori of
wardrobes of Barbie doll, her friends & family from 1959 to 1967-
81/2x11-256 Pgs.-(HB)

3787   **Blue Book of Dolls & Values** -11th Ed.Fowlke-Completely   17.95
revised-307 f/color photos-51/2x81/2-368 Pgs

1529   **Collector's Ency. of Barbie Dolls** -DeWein-Over 850 pho-   19.95
tos including 68 in full color-Very informative text- Complete
descriptions-1994 values-81/2x11-305 Pgs.-(HB)

2211   **Collector's Ency. of Madame Alexander Dolls** -Smith-   24.95
100's of full color photos-Complete descriptions-1994 values-
81/2x11-264 Pgs.-(HB)

2382   **Advertising Dolls-Id & Values** -Robison-1994 values-1000's of   9.95
listings-51/2x81/2-328 Pgs (P&I)

2082   **Collector's Guide to Magazine Paper Dolls** -Young-100's of   14.95
photos w/current values-81/2x11-160 Pgs.

1891   **French Dolls In Color, 3rd Series** -Smith-Over 30 different   14.95
mfgs.-Full color-81/2x11-160 Pgs.

2185   **Modern Collector's Dolls I** -Smith-1,000 photos-2,000 1991   17.95
values-309 Pgs.

2344   **Patricia Smith's Album of All Bisque Dolls** -100's of dolls in   14.95
f/color-Current values-104 Pgs.-81/2x11

2325   **Shirley Temple Dolls, Vol. I** -Smith-Loaded with photos &   17.95
1992 values-81/2x11

2084   **Teddy Bears, Annalee's & Steiff Animals** -3rd Series-   19.95
Mandel-No repeats of Volumes I or II-512 color photos-(HB)

TOYS & POP CULTURE

2060   **Pedal Cars, 1884-1970's** -Wood-Pedal Cars, Sleds, Scooters,   29.95
Tricycles & more-Current values-81/2x11

1514   **Character Toys & Collectibles** -Longest-Over 400 beautiful   19.95
full color photos-1992 values-(HB)

2184   **Coll. Guide to Cartoon & Promotional Drinking Glasses**   17.95
-Hervey-3,000+ glasses with values

Price

PRICE GUIDES ON COLLECTIBLES

Cat#   Price

2151 **Coll. Guide to Tootsietoys** -Richter-300+ Full-size examples   16.95
photo'd in f/color-1993 values

2021 **Coll. Male Action Figures** - G.I. Joe, Captain Action, Ken-   14.95
Manos-250 f/color photos-1992 values

2293 **Coll. Toy Trains** -Id. & V.G., 3rd Ed.-O'Brien-Illus.-Includes   22.95
Lionel, Amer. Flyer, Ives, Marx, etc.-81/2x11-340

3918 **Collecting Little Golden Books** -2nd Ed.-Santi-100's of   22.95
additions-81/2x11-266 Pgs.

3386 **Collecting Toy Soldiers** -2nd Edition-O'Brien-100's of photos   29.95
& current values-8 pgs. of color-81/2x11

3446 **Collecting Toys** 6th Edition-O'Brien-Greatly expanded-   22.95
81/2x11-586 Pgs.

2046 **Collector's Ency. of Toys & Banks** -Cranmer-1993 values-   14.95
81/2x11-218 Pgs.

2338 **Collector's Encyclopedia of Disneyana** -Longest-Stern-Two   24.95
toy experts working together to produce this all new book-850+
full color photos-Current values-81/2x11-224 Pgs.-(HB)

2249 **Comic Book Price Guide 1994** -24th Ed.-Overstreet-Every   15.00
known comic book from 1901 to present

2358 **Fisher Price Toys** -2nd Ed.-Murray-Revised, beautiful full   24.95
color-Current values

3334 **Lunch Boxes** -Aikins-500+lunch boxes-Pictorial & priced-   19.95
51/2x81/2-212 Pgs.

1540 **Modern Toys 1930-1980** -Baker-Full color-Includes Star   19.95
Wars-260 Pgs.-1993 values

2333 **Antique & Collectible Marbles** -3rd Edition-Grist-100's of   9.95
full color examples-Includes 1992 values for virtually every type
marble ever produced-A very popular title-51/2x81/2-96 Pgs.

2028 **Toys, Antique & Collectible** -Longest-Over 10,000 listings with 14.95
1994 values-Antique & modern toys-81/2x11-240 Pgs.

COWBOY & INDIAN COLLECTIBLES

2279 **Indian Artifacts of the Midwest** -Hothem-100's of photos-   14.95
Complete text including histories, descriptions & 1994 values-
One of our bestselling Indian books-81/2x11-192 Pgs.

1964 **Indian Axes & Related Stone Artifacts** -Hothem-Includes   14.95
histories & the future of axe collecting-1994 values

3805 **North American Indian Artifacts** -5th Ed.-Hothem-Completely   22.95
revised-100's of photo,Now 81/2x11-512 Pgs.s

1426 **Arrowheads & Projectile Points** -Hothem-Contains 100's of   7.95
photos with information about geographic origin, sizes, section
on detecting fakes & 1993 values-51/2x81/2-192 Pgs.

ADVERTISING COLLECTIBLES

1687 **Ant. Advertising Ency., Vol II** -Klug-No repeats-105 pgs. full 39.95
color-1,200 listings-240 Pgs. (HB)

2250 **Collector's Guide to Key-Wind Coffe Tins** -Stahl-100's of   19.95
photos, some color-Current values-81/2x11-172 Pgs.

3427 **Advertising Character Collectibles** -Dotz-Over 400 color   17.95
photos-includes 100's of characters-includes McDonald's, Ev-
eready, California Raisins-8 1/2x11-160 Pgs.

PRICE GUIDES ON COLLECTIBLES

2215   **Goldstein's Coca-Cola Collectibles** -Goldstein's 4 volume set   16.95
now in one volume-1993 values-F/C

9901   **Handbook of American Cigar Boxes** Classic history of the   16.95
Cigar Box as retail packaging. 176 pages-190 B&W photos-
indexed-includes 1994-95 prices (HB)

1922   **Standard Old Bottle Price Guide** -Sellari-Includes current   14.95
values-81/2x11-176 Pgs.

SPORTS COLLECTIBLES

2183   **Collecting Baseball Player Autographs** -Raycraft-Includes   9.95
100's of autographs & 1991 values

2276   **Decoys** -Kangas-600+ photos, some in f/color-Comprehesive   24.95
text is an invaluable reference-11x81/2-336 Pgs.

1559   **Encyclopedia of Golf Collectibles** -Olman-Over 2,000 items   14.95
listed-81/2x11-320 Pgs.

3361   **Coll. Ant. Bird Decoys & Duck Calls** -2nd Ed.-Luckey-230+   22.95
decoys & 100 calls shown-Current values-240 Pgs.

2287   **Fishing Tackle Ant. & Coll** -White-7,000+ items prices-1992   29.95
values-81/2x11-302 Pgs.

3731   **Florence's Standard Baseball Card Price Guide** -1994   9.95
6th Ed.-65,000 listings & current values-Simple to use-Cards in
alphabetical order-Full color identification-51/2x81/2-576 Pgs

3785   **Golf Antiques & Other Treasures of rht Game** -Olman-700+   19.95
photos-Forward by Hale Irwin-81/2x11-304 Pgs.

2194   **Old Fishing Lures & Tackle, 3rd Ed.** -Luckey-Completely   22.95
revised-472 Pgs. 81/2x11

3910   **Sports Americana Baseball Card Price Guide** -1994 16th   16.95
Ed.-Beckett-Illus.-6x9-1000 Pgs.-Over 300,000 prices

2349   **Value Guide to Baseball Collectibles** -Raycraft-1,000's of   16.95
listings w/current values-100's/photos-81/2x11-216 Pgs.

MISCELLANEOUS COLLECTIBLES

2214   **Huxford's Old Book Value Guide** - -3rd Ed.-25,000+ listings-   19.95
Totally different from Vol. I or II-Produced to be a companion
volume & not a revised edition-81/2x-11-408 Pgs.-(HB)

2368   **Amer. Prem. Guide to Knives & Razors** -3rd Ed.-Sargent-   22.95
Some color-1,000's of b&w photos-81/2x11-474 Pgs.

2386   **American Premium Record Guide** -4th Ed.-Docks-Id. & value   22.95
guide to 78's, 45's & LP's from 1900-1965

1868   **Antique Tools, Our American Heritage** -McNerney-1993   9.95
values-51/2x81/2-153 Pgs.

1714   **Black Collectibles** -Gibbs-500 full color photos-1993 values-   19.95
81/2x11-296 Pgs.-(HB)

2387   **Classic TV's-Pre War thru 1950's** -Wood-Current values-   16.95
81/2x11-86 Pgs.

2196   **Collecting Transistor Novelty Radios** -Breed-Full color-   24.95
Current values-81/2x11-217 Pgs.

2336   **Collector's Guide to Antique Radios** -2nd Ed.-Bunis-Over   17.95
600 all new photos-Includes over 5,000 sets with model#, descriptions & current values between 1920 & 1960-One of our
most popular titles-81/2x11-216 Pgs.

PRICE GUIDES ON COLLECTIBLES

Cat#		Price
1441	**Collector's Guide to Post Cards** -Wood-2,000 cards illus.-16 Color Pgs.-1993 values	9.95
2311	**Evolution of the Bicycle** -Wood-100's of photos-some color-Current valus-81/2x11-204 Pgs.	29.95
3854	**Hummel Figurines & Plates** -10th Ed.-Luckey-1,000's of Hummels-Current values-Fully illustrated-433 Pgs.	22.95
3820	**Huxford's Old Book Value Guide** -1994 6th Ed.-Almost 400 pgs. listing nearly 25,000 titles- any repeats of previous editions-81/2x11-384 Pgs. (HB) A bestseller.	19.95
3801	**2 Volume Set of Huxford's Standard Fine Art Value Guide** -Vols. I & II-81/2x11-(HB)	59.90
3921	**Huxford's Paperback Value Guide** -25,000 listings w/current values-Companion to Huxford's Old Book-352 Pgs. (HB)	19.95
1966	**Huxford's Standard Fine Art Value Guide I** -Over 30,000 listings-Current values-81/2x11-560 Ogs,-(HB)	29.95
2085	**Huxford's Standard Fine Art Value Guide, Vol. II Totally new-25,000+ listings & 1989 values-924 Pgs.-(HB)** Huxford's Standard Fine Art Value Guide, Vol. II Totally new-25,000+ listings & 1989 values-924 Pgs.-(HB)	29.95
2332	**Juke Boxes & Slot Machines** -3rd Ed.-Ayliffe-Includes gumball, trade simulators & arcade machines	14.95
3320	**Modern Guns, Identification & Values** -9th Ed.-Quertermous-Over 2,200 guns listed with current values-1,800+ illustrations-Important facts are given for each listing-81/2x11-480 Pgs.	12.95
2026	**Railroad Collectibles, 4th Ed.** -Baker-From China to Switch Keys-1993 values-81/2x11-176 Pgs.	14.95
2346	**Sheet Music Reference & Price Guide** -Pafik & Guiheen-250+ photos-Over 13,000 descriptions & current values of sheet music-A very informative & useful guide-81/2x11-292 Pgs.	18.95

REFERENCE (no prices)

Cat#		Price
2006	**Dictionary of Pottery & Porcelain Marks** -Kovel-5,000 marks-Pre 1850-(HB)	12.95
2071	**Kovel's American Silver Marks** , 1650 to the Present-10,000+ silversmiths listed-8x10-421 Pgs.-(HB)	40.00
1735	**Kovel's New Dictionary of Marks-Pottery & Porcelain** -1850 to present-290 Pgs.-(HB)	18.00
2379	**Lehner's Ency. of U.S. Marks on Pottery, Porcelain & Clay** -Lehner-Over 1,900 companies with over 8,000 marks, logos, symbols, etc. including old folk potteries, studio potters, manufacturers-81/2x11-644 Pgs.-(HB)	24.95
2236	**Art Pottery of the United States** -Evans-Very large text & histories-Some color	25.00

Other Price Guides

Catalog#_____

Book Title_____

_____ Price $_____

Catalog#_____

Book Title_____

_____ Price $_____

Catalog#_____

Book Title_____

_____ Price $_____

Total for Books $_____

CA res. add 8 1/4% sales tax $_____

Shipping @$4 each book $_____

TOTAL $_____

Date_____

Name (print)_____

Address_____

_____

MC/VISA#_____ Exp. date_____

Signature_____

Telephone (_____)_____

Send to: **Treasure Hunt Books**
Box 3028, Pismo Beach, CA 93448
Phone: (805) 773-6777

For Faster Service

FAX Credit Card Orders to: (805) 773-8436

Save $5...Save $20
Special to our valued readers

SAVE $5...Give this valuable book to a friend and we'll pay the postage. YOU SAVE $5. Pay only $24.95

Save $20...Got two friends you want to make rich? Save even more! Two copies shipped for only $39.90.

Other Price Guides

Catalog#_____

Book Title_____

_____Price $_____

Catalog#_____

Book Title_____

_____Price $_____

Catalog#_____

Book Title_____

_____Price $_____

Total for Books $_____

CA res. add 8 1/4% sales tax $_____

Shipping @$4 each book $_____

TOTAL $_____

Date_____

Name (print)_____

Address_____

_____

MC/VISA#_____Exp. date_____

Signature_____

Telephone (   )_____

Send to: **Treasure Hunt Books**
Box 3028, Pismo Beach, CA 93448
Phone: (805) 773-6777

For Faster Service

FAX Credit Card Orders to: (805) 773-8436

HANDBOOK OF
AMERICAN CIGAR BOXES

The fascinating story of the cigar box.
History's most important retail package!

From 1865-1920, four of five men smoked cigars. 1,500,000 brands vied for attention by packing their cigars in colorful and unusual boxes, now popular collector's items.

A valuable guideuseful to collectors, dealers, museums, historical societies, package designers, and all who want to relive the glories of 19th century advertising.

**Written by Dr. Tony Hyman
the national authority on
cigar industry history**

"The finest self-published book to cross my desk in years," said the head cataloger at the Library of Congress.

ISBN: 0-932780-00-8   c 1979

- **176 oversize pages**
- **Hard cover**
- **Printed to archival standards**
- **45,000 words of text**
- **190 large crisp photos**
- **Helpful charts and drawings**
- **Thoroughly indexed**
- **All new information, available nowhere else**
- **Includes 1994-95 Price Guide**
- **Signed and numbered**

"It's not often we rave about a book, but this deserves every accolade," said the editor of the Tin Can Collectors Association's newsletter.

Signed and numbered limited edition of 3,000; only 250 left. Order while still available.

Other Books by Tony Hyman

HYMAN'S TRASH OR TREASURE:
How to Find the Best Buyers of Antiques, Collectibles, and Other Undiscovered Treasures.

Everybody's Guide to 1,200 of the nation's top buyers has been brought together into a money making sourcebook by Dr. Tony Hyman, the national authority on buying and selling by mail. This directory gives you name, addresses and phone numbers of the most reliable specialty collectors and dealers...folks all over the U.S. and Canada ready to pay you cash for millions of items...by mail!

$29.95

THE WORLD'S MOST ACCURATE ANTIQUES & COLLECTIBLES PRICE GUIDE.

A Companion Publication for Hyman's Trash or Treasure
Over 5,000 Items priced according to what Buyers will actually pay.
No other price guide like it available.

$7.95

SELLAGRAMS.

A pad of 50 Easy-to-Use Forms for contacting Buyers.
Makes selling as easy as filling in the blanks. Assures you and the buyers that all basic information is being covered.

$4.95

Coming Soon

SECRETS OF
A MILLIONAIRE PICKER:
Inside Tips on How to Recognize Valuable
Collectibles As Told by the Experts

TONY LIVE!
"How to make more money faster and easier."
Video tape of Tony Hyman's
dynamic lecture at an antique dealers' conference

AUDIO TAPE SERIES

#1: Trash or Treasure: How you can put money
in your pocket by selling to collectors.

#2: Secrets of a Millionaire Picker, part I

BUYER'S PHONE BOOK

Pocket size phone book of important buyers
convenient for carrying on the road with you.

COMPLETE PROFESSIONAL KIT

Trash or Treasure
World's Most Accurate Price Guide
Secrets of a Millionaire Picker
Teaching Audio Tapes (2)
Supply of 50 Sellagrams
Patent Number to Date Translator
Buyer's Phonebook
plus more

Treasure Hunt Publications
Box 3028, Pismo Beach, CA 93448
(805) 773-6777